I've been ministering and p_____
tury and this is the most profo_____
read. The magnitude of this bo_____
scribe. It is a treasure of truth. Every chapter is w_____
Martin Luther said, "The Cross alone is our theology." Bob Sorge's
writing proves that reality.

Don Wilkerson
Co-Founder, Teen Challenge

The cross is the beauty of God put on display. At a time when
we need a clear sound, Bob calls us to the honor of gazing on the
glorious cross of Christ.

Stuart Greaves
International House of Prayer, Kansas City, Missouri

The Holy Spirit once whispered to me, "A cross-less Christianity
is satanic at its core." When Peter tried to convince Jesus He could
get to His destiny without the cross, Jesus responded sharply, "Get
behind Me, Satan, for you are not mindful of the things of God but
of men." I believe a gospel message without the cross will set many
up for a great exposing in the days ahead. Thank God for Bob Sorge
and this prophetic book to realign our lives to the cross!

Corey Russell
Author, *Teach Us to Pray*

What Bob's book *Secrets of the Secret Place* is to prayer, this
book is to our journey of maturing in love for Jesus. Important.
Formative. My hope is that every reader will engage in a fresh way
with renewed faith and hope in the journey where the love of Jesus
is taking them.

David Sliker
President, International House of Prayer University
Kansas City, Missouri

Editor: Edie Mourey
Cover designers: Marci Sorge, Jessica Beedle
Typesetter: Dale Jimmo

International Standard Book Number: 978-937725-59-4

Stay connected with us at:
YouTube.com/bobsorge
Instagram: bob.sorge
Store: www.oasishouse.com
Blog: bobsorge.com
twitter.com/BOBSORGE
Facebook.com/BobSorgeMinistry

About the CROSS Film Series: Your study group can watch Bob Sorge teach a nine-part video series on the content of this book. Find it at www.YouTube.com/bobsorge

Contents

CHAPTER ONE

Crux of the Matter

Two thousand years ago, a bloody execution site in Jerusalem became the heart of everything we believe and hold dear. It's utterly preposterous to the natural mind, but that's where God died. When Paul said, "We preach Christ crucified" (1 Cor 1:23), he indicated that we could take all the archives of Christian wisdom and reduce it to one essential: *the cross of Christ.*

I can't conceive a greater honor than to direct your meditations to this cross. Let's go there together, stand before Him in wonder, and worship. Behold the iron nails in each hand and foot. Look at the thorns hammered into His skull. Observe His skin and flesh flayed open and scourged raw. He's gasping and jerking in contorted spasms. People are mocking, and demons are raging. Plus, He's quaffing the cup of the Father's wrath against sin.

When the cross is before us, there's no place else to look.

This slab of wood that's hosting our Savior's convulsions is the centerpiece of our faith. It's where the Carpenter from Nazareth, after a three-year teaching hiatus, returned to His woodworking profession. Taking a beam in hand, He went to work and crafted our salvation.

Actually, He came to earth to die. Why? Because we were held captive by sin and Satan and condemned to death. We were helpless to deliver ourselves, so He came to the rescue. With infinite love, He planned our prison break and broke us free.

If you're not captive to sin and don't need to be saved, then I suppose you're good to go. But if you need saving, the cross is the best news ever!

Why is the cross at the center of our faith? Because it's at the center of God's heart.

> The cross is God bridging every divide and bounding every hurdle to get to you with His salvation.

Center of God's Heart

To discover what someone feels most passionately about, ask about their highest joys and deepest sorrows. When they tell you, their cheeks will flush, their eyes will flame, and their words will tumble. So go ahead and ask Him, "What do You feel most strongly about? What's at the center of Your heart?"

I'm persuaded there's nothing God feels more passionately about than His Son's cross. Never before or since has anything lacerated His heart so deeply. He watched Him endure unimaginable horror, but more than that, He suffered with Him. And He'll *never* forget.

The cross is God's most memorable event ever. He has deeper convictions and stronger opinions about Calvary than any other topic. Come to the cross and you get God's most ponderous passions. The cross is *our* center because it's *His* center.

The cross was also Paul's center, for he told the Corinthian church, "For I determined not to know anything among you except Jesus Christ and Him crucified" (1 Cor 2:2). While in Corinth, the cross was the center of his preaching. Paul affirmed the same preaching emphasis among the churches of Galatia when he asked them, "Who has bewitched you that you should not obey the truth, before whose eyes Jesus Christ was clearly portrayed among you as crucified?" (Gal 3:1). It seems that Christ crucified was the center of Paul's message everywhere he went.

Let's make it our center, too.

It's not just that the cross is in *our* crosshairs; we're also in *His* crosshairs. The cross placed us at God's center. It revealed that the human race is the axis of His universe. I mean, to how many other planets in the universe has Jesus gone and gotten Himself crucified? You'd think ours is the only planet God sees. It seems He can't peel His eyes off us. O the tender and compassionate mercies of our heavenly Father! The fact is, we're *chosen*, and we can't get away from it.

Calvary signifies there's no escaping the fixated gaze of an irreversibly invested God.

Our Center

The cross is the stent at the heart of our faith. Discard the cross and you may as well chuck your Bible and pitch your faith. Toss the cross and you jettison Jesus. No cross no Jesus. Receive it, though, and you get all of God.

It's the genesis of our faith, our love, and our life. It's the launch point for all we hold dear. Everything starts here. If they take everything else from us but leave us with the cross, it's enough.

A crossless Christianity is a farce, a sham, a fake, a scam. It was Jesus' pathway to the Father, and it's ours, too. The way to the Father is as narrow as the wood on which Christ was crucified.

Don't let anyone swindle you out of the cross. Without it you have nothing, but with it you have everything.

We took *crux*, the Latin word for *cross*, and pasted it into our English dictionary. It means *the decisive or most important point at issue*. The cross of Christ is the crux—the most important matter at hand. Though we might stray at times, we keep returning to the crux of the matter over and over.

John said they also crucified two thieves that day, with "Jesus in the center" (John 19:18). This much hasn't changed: We still have *"Jesus in the center."* We're never truer to our faith than when fixated upon our center—the cross of Christ.

Throughout this book, I'm going to defend the premise that the cross is the central pillar of our faith. For starters, consider that:

- It's the theme of the first Bible book written (the book of Job).
- It's the recurring theme in Genesis.

> When a conversation becomes combative, allow the irrefutable wisdom of the cross to defuse the debate.

(God sacrificed animals to clothe Adam and Eve; He predicted Calvary in Genesis 3:15; the Genesis 22 story on Mt. Moriah was all about Calvary; so too was God's burning-oven covenant with Abraham in Genesis 15.)

- It was the message of Moses' sacrificial system.
- Many of the Psalms foretell and emote the sufferings of the Messiah.
- The prophets were distracted with the sufferings of Christ (e.g., Isa 53).
- It was the center of Paul's preaching and the recurring theme of his writings.
- The wisdom of the cross answers all the social issues of today's world.
- Major life decisions come into focus through the cross.
- It makes sense of life's trials.
- The Lord's Supper places it at the center of our worship.
- Jesus is a resurrected Lion, but the focus of heaven's worship is on the Lamb who prevailed on the cross (Rev 5:12).

The cross is our center.

Jesus' First Sermon

In His first sermon—commonly called *the Sermon on the Mount*—Jesus placed the cross squarely at the center of His teachings. He began with nine *Beatitudes*. His listeners didn't know it, but He was actually prophesying blessing over His upcoming crucifixion. See how blessed the crucified Christ truly was:

"Blessed are the poor" (Matt 5:3)—He died penniless, naked and destitute—and now owns everything.

"Blessed are those who mourn" (Matt 5:4)—according to Isaiah 53:3-4, Jesus was a Man of sorrows who bore our griefs and carried our sorrows on the cross. He is comforted now with exceeding joy.

"Blessed are the meek" (Matt 5:5)—that the Son of God would die on a cross is consummate meekness, and now He has inherited the whole earth.

"Blessed are those who hunger and thirst for righteousness" (Matt 5:6)—surely He was blessed when on the cross He cried, *I thirst!* Rivers of living water now flow from His throne.

"Blessed are the merciful" (Matt 5:7)—by dying in our place, Jesus was extravagantly merciful to each of us and is now blessed because of it.

"Blessed are the pure in heart" (Matt 5:8)—our Pureheart died a spotless, blameless Lamb, and now all creation blesses the Lamb of God.

"Blessed are the peacemakers" (Matt 5:9)—Jesus is the ultimate Peacemaker who, in the words of Ephesians 2:14, became our peace so we could be reconciled to God.

"Blessed are those who are persecuted for righteousness' sake" (Matt 5:10)—beyond all argument, Jesus was crucified for righteousness' sake (and is now blessed forever).

"Blessed are you when they revile and persecute you, and say all kinds of evil against you falsely. Rejoice and be exceedingly glad, for great is your reward in heaven, for so they persecuted the prophets who were before you" (Matt 5:11-12)—in this final Beatitude, Jesus described His cross perfectly, where they said all kinds of evil against Him falsely. Therefore, all the rewards of the Beatitudes are His in their fullness—blessed be His name forever and ever!

Just as Jesus was blessed through His cross, the blessings of the Beatitudes are also bestowed on those who take up their cross and follow Him. From the very start of His teaching ministry, He sought to strengthen our hearts with confidence so we would boldly share in the blessings of His cross.

If you have a message that has no room for the cross, we have no room for your message.

A Call to the Center

I'm calling us back to our center. Preachers, let's place the cross at the center of our preaching. Worship leaders, make the cross the center of our singing. Songwriters, craft songs with lyrics that laud the Lamb. There are *thousands* of songs about the cross yet to be written—give them to us!

I call on every precious believer to place the cross at the center of your thoughts and affections. You'll never graduate past nor outgrow the cross. Put that middle cross back at the center and keep returning to it over and over. Why? Because it's at God's center, and is central to everything we hold dear.

Christ crucified is our wisdom, power, vitality, and life. We remember, and we're coming back. *Holy Lamb of God, You're the reason for everything we do!*

For Group Study and Discussion *

1. Read Matthew 26-28 this week, and share with the group what moved you most in this reading of the crucifixion account.

2. What do you suppose the Father was thinking as He watched Jesus on the cross? Can you think of a Scripture that reveals a little bit of what was going on in His heart? Talk about it.

3. Read 1 Corinthians 1:18-2:8. How central do you think the cross should be to our messaging? How well are we doing this? Talk about the author's premise that the cross is the central pillar of our faith.

4. "No cross no Jesus." What does that statement mean to you?

5. In what ways do you see the cross in the Old Testament?

6. Which three statements in this chapter meant the most to you? Why?

7. As you close your group time, center your prayers around 1 Corinthians 1:23-24.

* Note: Your group can watch Bob Sorge teach a nine-part video series on the content of this book. Find it at www.YouTube.com/bobsorge

CHAPTER TWO

It Calibrates Us

The cross calibrates us. Just as measuring instruments (such as scales) need to be calibrated repeatedly so that their measurements are accurate, our lives need to be continually calibrated to the cross. Over and over, we revisit whether our lifestyles and values line up with Christ and Him crucified.

Every believer knows what it's like to take a stand in values and beliefs only to feel the eroding waves of everyday life trying to wash them away. The cross is a safeguard that helps us preserve truth, integrity, wise priorities, and proper values.

The cross aligns and keeps us true to Christ. Its standard is precisely the chiropractic adjustment we need to remain upright.

Have you ever gone to a grocery store's fresh produce section and tried to weigh your fruit on the scales only to discover the scales were off center and unreliable? In a similar way, our hearts often stray to the left or right, and we must return over and over to the central standard of the cross.

Knocked Off Center

When we deviate, what must we do to align again with the cross-centric kingdom of God? Get *violent*. Jesus told us, "The kingdom of heaven suffers violence, and the violent take it by force" (Matt 11:12). Staying centered on the cross means war. Returning the conversation to the cross involves violence. If you think I'm exaggerating, An alliance of opposing forces resist us when we resolve to center on the cross. For starters, the first enemy we'll encounter is the devil. He'll do anything to divert our attention in any other direction. Some of his devices include:

- Temptation: He'll tempt us to sin

> The cross calibrates your theology.

because disobedience spins us away from the cross.

- Accusation: He'll tell us we're unworthy to approach the cross, but the blood of Christ is the very thing that silences him (Rev 12:11).
- Deception: He'll use lies to get our focus on something other than the cross. When we renew our minds in the truth of God's word, the lies are exposed and we're restored to the cross (Rom 12:1-2).
- Distraction: Satan will use anything and everything to get us off center, but a return to the cross will focus our hearts on our first love.
- Discouragement: When Satan uses adversity to try to overwhelm you with hopelessness, the cross will calibrate your faith and replenish your courage.
- Futility: Satan will try to entice us with the frivolous and divert our attention onto things that are temporary and trite. The cross restores our sobriety and reorients us to the eternal.

The last thing the enemy wants you to do is fix the cross firmly at the center of your affections and thoughts.

A second enemy of the cross is our flesh. It recoils at the cross. Let's be honest—there's something in our flesh that doesn't even want to read a book on the cross. You've probably used kingdom violence just to open this book, and you'll probably need to declare war on your flesh if you're to read it all the way to the end. But if you do, the message of the cross has the power to be altogether *lifechanging*.

Okay, as the author of this book, let me talk about my flesh. Something in *my* flesh has resisted writing this book. There's a marketing mouth somewhere in my carnal mind that's saying, *Nobody has a felt need to buy a book on the cross. This book will sit in the warehouse. Why am I wasting my time writing a book nobody will read, anyway?*

Okay, here comes full disclosure. I encounter resistance every time I go to preach on the cross. And I've learned from other preachers that I'm not alone in this struggle. What's the nature of the resistance? Well, I don't have the animal entirely cornered and identified yet, but am I engaging principalities and powers in heavenly places (Eph 6:12)? Are demons assigned to resist the proclamation of the cross? I reckon that's part of it. But I think there's something else going on, too.

Something in my flesh doesn't want to preach on the cross. There, I said it. I know the cross is the central event of our faith, and yet something in my soul resists going there. Here's my best guess at what's going on. I think I hesitate because my flesh wants listeners to applaud my preaching and go, "Great message!" But after a sermon on the cross, people rarely go, "That was great. Please give us more!"

Something in my flesh wants people impressed with my preaching, but you can't preach on the cross and come away looking good. People are too distracted by the enormity of the silhouette to pay attention to the smoothness of the delivery. The cross is so massive it dwarfs everything in its orb, preacher included.

I think most believers experience a version of this same struggle. Something in our flesh resists inserting the cross into everyday conversation. To do so requires kingdom violence because nothing in the world supports that narrative. They'll look at you like, *Why did you just say that? We weren't talking about the cross.*

Our flesh doesn't want to calibrate to the cross because, to hold to the crucified life, we must exercise bold violence. You can feel your flesh pulling away from the nails. It seems that all our enemies—the devil, the world, the culture, the cares of life, and the flesh—conspire to draw us off center.

One day we knelt at the cross; how is it, then, that it's no longer upon our tongue? How did our flesh ever manage to crawl off the cross in the first place? I compel you, beloved soldier, to thrust the

When it came to killing God, the social liberals and social conservatives finally found something they could agree on.

cross again through your flesh and cement it deeply in the moorings of all your affections and aspirations. Be violent, dear friend of the cross, and erect it again large in your heart.

Minimizing Forces in the Church

Nobody is surprised that the devil and our flesh would resist the preaching of the cross. But now I turn to something more difficult to address—forces *within the church* that sometimes curb the visibility we grant the cross in our emphasis and witness. I'll mention a few of those forces.

Tradition. I'm a preacher's kid, and I grew up in a Pentecostal church tradition in which the cross received little mention. For example, in our denomination it was customary to hear a sermon about the triumphal entry on Palm Sunday and then a sermon about the resurrection of Christ the following Easter Sunday. Between those two Sundays was an event that didn't get a lot of press. The cross was relegated to a Communion service on Good Friday and was typically attended by a nucleus of the most devout. Why so little mention? Did we not know what to say about the cross?

Missiology. Missions movements have historically struggled to find effective ways to reach people in Arab nations with the gospel. In response, some missiologists have come to believe that the preaching of the cross in Arab nations actually undermines the effectiveness of our witness. They say that the cross offends people in that part of the world and that, if we want to win them, we should speak rather of Jesus' teachings and miracles. These missiologists unapologetically advise today's evangelists to be minimalists on the cross.

~ *Doctrine.* Certain doctrines in the church today validate the minimizing of the cross. For example, there's a sinister doctrine circulating today that says the cross took place under the old covenant. According to this doctrine, the teachings and life of Christ all took place under the old covenant and as such hold secondary authority in the life of the believer. The proponents of this doctrine claim that the new covenant didn't officially launch until the resurrection of Jesus and the outpouring of the Spirit at Pentecost (Acts 2), and everything pre-resurrection was old covenant. They make the grave error of drawing the new covenant line at the wrong place. In contrast, Scripture draws the line at John the Baptist, telling us that the new gospel era began with John (Mark 1:1-2; Luke 16:16). One of these teachers falsely claims that the New Testament epistles such as Romans hold supremacy over the words of Christ in the four Gospels. Here's my take on it:

- <u>Shun</u> any teaching that lessens the importance of the cross by placing it in the old covenant era.

I posted a comment about the cross on social media on one occasion, and someone responded: "The focus should never stay on the cross." That sentiment is actually not altogether uncommon in the church. There are doctrinal orientations in some quadrants of the church that seek to move past the cross and settle entirely on the resurrection. I'm a lover of the resurrection, as was Paul, but he wrote, "We preach Christ crucified, to the Jews a stumbling block and to the Greeks foolishness, but to those who are called, both Jews and Greeks, Christ the power of God and the wisdom of God" (1 Cor 1:23-24). The cross isn't something to move past. It's our center.

Christ crucified is both "the power of God and the wisdom of God" (1 Cor 1:24). What sinister motive, therefore, would cause us to set aside our power and wisdom? How crazy would that be? To what can I compare this madness? Minimizing the cross is just about as crazy as:

- A basketball coach benching his star player during the biggest game of the year. How crazy is that?
- A general sending his troops to the front lines without ammunition.

> Pilate thought Jesus was on trial, but Jesus knew Pilate was on trial.

How crazy is that?

- McDonalds deciding to stop serving Big Macs. How crazy is that?

To give the cross secondary visibility is *lunacy*.

It's time to recalibrate. When we place the cross at the center of our preaching, listeners find the keys to the greatest issues of life. When we recalibrate our homes and make the cross once again the centerpiece of everyday life, our families become havens of health. Whether at school or work, on social media, or with friends, talk about the cross. Allow it to inform, shape, and direct the conversation.

Back to the Beginning

When a seed is germinated, procreative life is released and gestation commences. This is where the primal forces of life are actuated. To reclaim the vitality of a thing, therefore, we often return to its inception. Let me show a few ways we pay attention to this principle.

When we want to renew the passion of marriage, sometimes we revisit the things that brought us together in the first place. Or, if a local church has lost its relevance, it might want to dust off its founding vision. Or, if a business is struggling, it might need to be reminded of the passion behind its initial launch.

Jesus drew on this principle when asked by the Pharisees whether He was okay with divorce. To answer their question, He took them back to the moment when marriage was first instituted. When God ordained the institution of marriage in the beginning, there was no provision for divorce—because when marriage is preserved in its pristine beauty and integrity, there is no divorce. Jesus was affirming that, to reclaim the vitality of marriage, we should return to its beginning.

This principle is also true regarding our faith. To recover the vitality of Christianity, we should return to its inception. Where did it all start? *The cross.* When we kneel again in blood and water, we recover the simplicity, purity, and power of our faith.

The same can be said for our worship. To find renewed vitality in worship, go back to the beginning. Where did it start? Well, if you follow the river of worship all the way back to its headwaters, you'll be standing at the cross.

Christ crucified is the source, inspiration, and fountainhead of worship. That's where the two of you first met. You'll recover your first love by returning to the place where your love was first kindled (Rev 2:4). With every return visit, you excavate love's passions and redig the wells of gratefulness, abandonment, and loyalty. *amen !*

Sometimes worship leaders struggle to find corporate momentum in the Spirit when leading a congregation in worship. When they ask me what to do, my answer is usually, *Take us back to the cross.* That's where tears flow, hearts warm, and spirits soar. The cross lifts every head, every eye, and every heart. It's the genesis and fountainhead of love—an inexhaustible treasure trove for the language of love. A return to the cross opens unquenchable fires and unending love songs.

Songwriters, you're going to write your best love songs by stationing at the cross. Here, love inspires love; abandonment empowers abandonment; longing fuels longing; zeal ignites zeal; deeps calls unto deep; tears beget tears. The best songs about the cross have yet to be written.

Stop once more and behold your crucified Savior. Gaze on His hands, feet, brow, and pierced side. Whisper your gratitude, and let the fountains of affection flow.

The cross is the alpha and omega of worship—which means it's not only where worship starts but also where it ends. When I say worship ends with the cross, I have an end-time meaning in mind. When John saw worship at the end of the age, he saw all creation gathered

Knowing that Judas would betray Him, Jesus washed his feet. This is how we serve those who ha...

round *the Lamb.* With every eye fixated on Him, every creature was saying, "Worthy is the Lamb who was slain to receive power and riches and wisdom, and strength and honor and glory and blessing!" (Rev 5:12).

Like many things, worship has a tendency to get weird and imbalanced. All too easily, <u>congregational worship</u> becomes about music, platforms, screens, lights, careers, screenshots, profiles, egos, and income streams. The whole thing <u>must get calibrated</u>, over and over, to the cross—where all the accoutrements fall away and our gaze remains on only one thing— <u>"a Lamb as though it had been slain"</u> (Rev 5:6).

It's time to return to the beginning, reclaim the vitality of our love, and center again on the middle cross. Only the crucified Christ can renew denominations, churches, families, and individuals. Let's galvanize a worldwide, revolutionary return to the cross and get centered again!

For Group Study and Discussion

1. In what ways have your recent meditations on the cross re-centered you?

2. Does your flesh recoil from approaching the cross? What does this tell you about yourself?

3. What kind of resistance do you face when you try to talk about the cross?

4. Three elements are mentioned within the church that seek to downplay the cross. In what way have you experienced any of this?

5. Christ crucified is both "the power of God and the wisdom of God" (1 Cor 1:24). What does that mean? What Scriptures support this idea?

6. If the cross is the fountainhead of worship, what are the implications for our worship in the church?

7. As you close your group time, center your prayers around Revelation 5:12.

CHAPTER THREE

Jesus' Most Common Teaching

A s Jesus moved from town to town, He often repeated His teachings. Why? To expose new audiences to His message, and to help His disciples remember His primary messages. Some were repeated more than others, and I'm persuaded there was one message He intentionally delivered more than any other.

Here's how I stumbled onto it. I was doing a word search in my Bible search program, and when I punched in the search phrase, my computer displayed verses from all four Gospels.

Now, people who study the Bible know this almost never happens. You rarely find the same content in all four Gospels. The reason? John.

John wrote his Gospel roughly thirty years after the other three evangelists. He knew what they had written, so in His account of Jesus' life and ministry, he intentionally penned things the others hadn't mentioned. He was trying to complement, not reiterate, what they had recorded.

That's why there's very little material common to all four Gospels. For example, there are only four stories found in all four Gospels: Jesus' baptism, the feeding of the five thousand, the triumphal entry, and the cross. Of Jesus' many predictions, only three are reiterated in all four Gospels: the prediction of Judas's betrayal, Peter's denial, and the passion.

Of Christ's many teachings, there's only *one* that's recorded in all four Gospels. Let me say a couple things about it to stir your curiosity. When you examine the context of each mention, you realize it's the only teaching Jesus delivered on *four different occasions.* All four mentions took place in the final year of His ministry which means, the closer He drew to Calvary, the more He spoke this word.

Furthermore, the topic of conversation on each occasion was different. Although the maxim given all four times was the same, Jesus' point each time was different—that is, how He applied the principle to His listeners' lives in each context was unique. This is important because it helps us see that this particular teaching applies to literally *every area of life.*

His most common teaching was the most universally relevant.

It was the most counterintuitive of all His axioms, and was only one verse in length. Again, I think it was His most common teaching.

While you're trying to think which dictum it might be, let me ask a couple questions.

If you knew there was one teaching that Jesus gave more than any other, would you pay it special attention? Would you be especially eager to obey it? Would you determine to never forget it? Would you want to make it a rule for all of life?

If *you* were writing the Bible and wanted to emphasize one statement of Christ's by placing it in all four Gospels, which one would *you* choose?

Okay, enough suspense. What was His most common teaching? Here it is: *Find your life you'll lose it; lose your life for My sake and you'll find it.*

It should still be our most common message—especially in these last days.

Four Different Occasions

Let's look at the four distinct occasions He spoke this word, and the meaning of His message each time.

The first occurrence was on Jesus' third tour of Galilee, recorded only by Matthew.

> He who finds his life will lose it, and he who loses his life for My sake will find it (Matt 10:39).

Sell Joseph for twenty pieces of silver and he'll "save many lives" (Gen 45:7). Sell Jesus for thirty pieces of silver and He'll do the same.

In context, Jesus was talking about how to handle the conflict when our loyalty to Him and family clash. He predicted that people in our own households would be hostile to us because of our loyalty to Him. His point was that, if we compromise our devotion to Him in order to keep peace in the family, we'll lose our lives. But if our loyalty to Him takes precedence over loyalty to parents or spouse or children, we'll find our lives.

Jesus' message at this first occurrence was this: Loyalty to family is noble, but loyalty to Him must supersede it.

The second occurrence of this axiom was on His visit to Caesarea Philippi and was recorded by the three Synoptic Gospel writers (Matt 16:25; Mark 8:35; Luke 9:24). Let's quote Mark's mention.

> For whoever desires to save his life will lose it, but whoever loses his life for My sake and the gospel's will save it (Mark 8:35).

In context, Jesus was telling His disciples for the first time of His upcoming suffering, death, and resurrection. Peter was so appalled at the notion that he actually rebuked Jesus for talking like that. In response, Jesus insisted that not only would this happen to Him, but it would also happen to anyone who wanted to come after Him. Every follower was invited to deny himself, take up his cross, and follow Him.

Jesus' message at this second occurrence was this: We're called to the crucified life. If they would lose their lives and take up their cross, they would save their lives.

The third occurrence of this proverb was on His final journey to Jerusalem. Luke alone recorded this one.

> Whoever seeks to save his life will lose it, and whoever loses his life will preserve it
> (Luke 17:33).

In context, Jesus was talking about the end times and that

we must guard our hearts lest we place our affections on earthly possessions. To illustrate His point, He used the graphic example of Lot's wife who lost her life in the overthrow of Sodom. She loved her city, and when the angels pulled her out of Sodom and tried to take her to safety, she turned reflexively and took one last look of longing at the city she enjoyed so much. Instantly, she became a pillar of salt (Gen 19:26).

Lot's wife represents the believer who loves Jesus and also the world. As a believer in God, she had many positive qualities: She supported true worship in her home; she was not an adulteress; she tended well to her home; she loved the market, the neighbors, her friends, and the culture of a prosperous society; she loved bright tapestries, quality garments, good food, good drink, the arts, and music; she was a believer who found joy and satisfaction in the natural things of this world. When urged to escape the world she knew, suddenly the true affections of her heart were exposed.

That's why Jesus warned us in the previous verse, "Remember Lot's wife" (Luke 17:32).

Jesus' message at this third occurrence was this: When He returns to earth for us, He doesn't want our souls so wrapped around the things of this world that, when He calls us up into the air to be with Him, we turn around and look back wistfully at all the things we're leaving behind. He wants to return for a bride who is so in love with Him that, when she sees His face, she'll never have a second thought about the home she's leaving behind. Her face will be fully set on the One she loves. Jesus made it clear that if, at His return, we eagerly leave all the stuff we've accrued in this life and cleave to Him, we'll preserve our lives forever.

The fourth occurrence of this teaching was during His final week of ministry in Jerusalem, just a couple days before Calvary. John alone recorded this one.

We'll be sprinkled with blood in the eternal city (Heb 12:24). The fountain Calvary opened, therefore, is *everlasting*.

He who loves his life will lose it, and he who hates his life in this world will keep it for eternal life (John 12:25).

In context, Jesus was saying that a seed must die for it to produce fruit. He was speaking of martyrdom and assured us that, if we would hate our life even unto death, we would keep it for eternal life. Jesus portrayed the death of a martyr as the dying of a seed that ultimately produces a great harvest. Tertullian supported this idea when he wrote, "The *blood of the martyrs is the seed of the Church.*"

Jesus didn't invite us to a life of comfort, ease, and self-actualization. He called us to die—to self, to sin, and to loving our life. He called us to hate our life so that we might gain it for eternal life. We embrace this hatred of the self-life when we follow Christ.

Again, on the four occasions Jesus delivered this precept, His point was different each time. That's because this precept applies to practically every area of daily life. It answers almost any dilemma or question. If you'll lose your life you'll find it; if you'll hate your life you'll gain it for eternal life. This wisdom was the core of Jesus' teachings.

Some Biblical Examples

We see this principle in several Bible stories. For example, Haman sought to save his life and lost it; in contrast, Esther willingly lost her life and saved it (Esther 4–6). In another story, Orpah saved her life and lost it; in contrast, Ruth lost her life and saved it (Ruth 1–4). In yet another story, Absalom loved his life and lost it; in contrast, David lost his life and gained it.

I'm so glad Jesus didn't come as the son of Absalom, grasping to gain His life; rather, He came as the son of David, seeking to lay His life down for the whole world. I'm taking my cues from Him.

Our heavenly Father is the best example of this maxim.

At the cross, the Father was losing His life by giving up His beloved Son; as a result, He gained His life forever by raising His Son back up and bringing redeemed humanity into the family. The cross is the most perfect revelation, therefore, of the heart of our Father. He's always laying His life down for His creation, that He might truly live. He's been doing this ever since the inception of creation, and He'll continue to do this for all eternity. It's just who He is.

We didn't really understand this part of the Father's heart until the cross. But suffering reveals. The sufferings of the cross revealed the generosity of our heavenly Father who is always losing His life for the sake of His children.

At Christ's passion, the disciples were tempted to save their lives. Jesus had warned them, "Watch and pray, lest you enter into temptation" (Matt 26:41). Instead of watching and praying, however, they slept. Thus, when the moment of temptation hit—that is, when Jesus was arrested and their arrest also seemed imminent—they all panicked, abandoned Him to His fate, and fled. They entered into the temptation of seeking to save their lives.

An anonymous poet compared Jesus Christ with Alexander the Great, the imperialistic Greek emperor who conquered over fifteen nations during the period 336–323 BC. You'll recognize that the poet had Christ's most common teaching in mind when he wrote this:

> Jesus and Alexander died at thirty-three;
> one lived and died for self,
> one died for you and me.
> One died upon a throne,
> the other on a cross;
> one's life a triumph seemed,
> the other's but a loss.
>
> One led vast armies forth,
> the other walked alone;
> one shed a whole world's blood,

> The cross reveals a Father who's suffering more than anyone can imagine, and always laying down His life for His creation.

the other gave His own.
One won the world in life,
and lost it all in death;
the other lost His life,
to win the whole world's faith.

Jesus and Alexander died at thirty-three;
one died in Babylon,
and one at Calvary.
One gained all for himself,
and one Himself He gave.
one conquered every throne,
the other every grave.[1]

The goal of the gospel is not to help us get our life back. Should we get it back, we'd just mess it up all over again. Rather, the goal of the gospel is to help us give our life away.

Jesus called us to lose our lives, even to the point of martyrdom. General Ferdinand Foch, the Supreme Allied Commander in World War I, is credited with the statement, *Battles are won by teaching soldiers how to die, not how to avoid dying.* Jesus taught us to die, and now nothing can stop His ever-expanding kingdom.

In your present season of life, is your favor with others growing or diminishing? How about your joy, your finances, or the peace in your family? Is the momentum around your life growing or diminishing? Either way, Jesus' counsel is the same: Hate your life. Lose your life.

Are you at an important crossroads? Are you facing a critical decision regarding your career, or education, or business venture, or investment opportunity, or spouse or children? Do you lack the wisdom to know what to do next? If so, let Jesus give you His angle on it: Hate your life, and you'll gain it for eternal life.

When someone asks you for advice, let this be your first answer: *Lose your life for the sake of Christ, so that you might*

1 Richard Wurmbrand, *The Oracles of God* (Bartlesville, OK: Living Sacrifice Book Company, 1995), 41.

preserve it. It's the best counsel you could ever give anyone.

Do you want to make a difference in your world? Do you want to do something great for the kingdom of God? Would you aspire to influence world history? Do you want to achieve great things and make a significant contribution to your generation? Do you want the smile of Jesus on all you do? Do you want to discover who you really are? Then hate your life. Lose your life and you'll find it.

According to our Master's wisdom, the only way to find your real identity is to lose it.

> Lose your life in fasting.
> Lose your life in giving.
> Lose your life in serving.
> Lose your life in prayer.
> Lose your life by preferring others.
> Lose your life by showing mercy.
> Lose your life in caring.
> Lose your life in helping.
> Lose your life in labor.
> Lose your life in study.
> Lose your life in another generation.
> Lose your life in the harvest.
> Lose your reputation.
> Lose your comforts.
> Lose your strength.
> Lose your rights.
> Lose your favor.
> Lose your following.
> Lose the argument.
> Lose the inheritance.

When we come to the cross, we're looking at a Man who practiced what He preached. Although He owned everything, He lost it all for our sakes. Because He had everything, He could die with nothing. He lost His life and found it forever.

The love of the cross "does not seek its

> The lower you lay your life down, the higher the Father can lift you.

own" (1 Cor 13:5). I hear His cross saying, *It's more blessed to give your life than to receive it.*

For all eternity, the Jesus we've fallen in love with is going to be losing His life for others. It's just who He is, and it's just what He does.

Because of Him, the same will also be true of us. Forever we'll be laying our lives down, always hating our lives so we can gain them for eternal life.

It's simply who we are—embodying the cross forever.

For Group Study and Discussion

1. Look up all the verses where Jesus told us to lose our lives, and then read the surrounding verses. What are your observations?

2. Can you identify some other teachings of Christ that were also counterintuitive?

3. How valuable has it been to you, to identify Jesus' most common teaching? What implications does this carry for your life?

4. Have you ever faced a situation where loyalty to God and loyalty to your family conflicted? Tell us about it.

5. Read Luke 17:32 and the surrounding verses. How is this passage relevant to you right now? What other Scriptures also speak to you about this?

6. What did Jesus mean when He told us to hate our lives?

7. As you close your group time, center your prayers around Matthew 10:39.

CHAPTER FOUR

Can You See It?

L et's devote ourselves to magnifying the cross. Make it large as you can. Speak of it often and make it your honor to incorporate it into everyday conversations. Talk about the blood, the wounds, the agony, the anguish. Talk about what Dubay called *consummate splendor in monstrous horror.*[1]

When the Moravians launched their missionary endeavors, they decided to take with them *blood and wounds theology*, meaning they made the sufferings of the cross the centerpiece of their message. Like Paul, they preached Christ and Him crucified (1 Cor 1:23). This emphasis on the bloody sacrifice of Christ carried them to the four corners of the earth and empowered their mission.

We should make the cross large—if anywhere—in our churches. In your church sanctuary, does your décor have room for a cross? I'm advocating for making it the center of both our message and media. For me, it's never large enough. It's impossible for you to place a cross in your church building that's too large for me because it's my *everything*.

The Cross Our Glory

My boast is in the cross of Christ (Gal 6:14). I wear its sufferings as my coat of arms and honor its blood as my banner. I'll never apologize for the cross. The wounds are my boast and the shame is my glory.

In Jesus' day, crucifixion was considered the most shameful, demeaning way for someone to die, but we're not ashamed of it. Jesus despised its shame (Heb 12:2), and so do we. He took something that was hideously abhorrent and, by making it His workbench, infused it with dignity, honor, and majesty.

> How do you give a lavish gift to a Son who already has everything? Find the answer and you'll be gazing at the majesty of the cross.

Now it's become our glory. It's the first thing on our minds and the closing thought of our conversations. We put it on our steeples and carry it around our necks. We hang it on our walls and print it on our logos. It's even on our tattoos.

O the wisdom of the cross! The world views it as foolishness, but to us it's the wisdom and power of God. The hidden wisdom of the cross is like an endless bank of gems and pearls yet to be discovered—and we're after them!

I'm stuttering right now to speak properly about something so sublime. How can I possibly do justice to its glorious grandeur with my vacuous vocabulary and pitiful pen?

The cross is the power of our gospel. Maybe this is why, at the time of this writing in 2020, the Communist government of China is forcibly removing crosses from the Christian churches of that great land. In honor of their Communist ideals, they want to eviscerate and cripple the power of the Jesus movement. But no atheist government can overcome the gospel of the cross. You can remove it from our buildings but not from our hearts.

As already mentioned, some missionary movements promote a minimalist approach to the cross, particularly among those seeking to reach Arab communities. They recommend we not mention the cross when witnessing to Arabs because it offends and repels them. I believe the intentions of those missionaries are sincere, but when we remove the cross from our witness, we lose the power of our gospel. No cross no miracles.

Samuel Zwemer and Leif Hetland have both testified that, when they took the gospel to predominantly Muslim nations, they found the cross pivotal in compelling their listeners to faith. Yes, the cross offended; but it also had an attractional power unmatched by any other element in the gospel.

The cross is our message for the world—we have no other.

Some theological camps minimize the cross because they suppose the crucified life contradicts the *more abundant life* that Christ promised in John 10:10. Wishing to emphasize the overcoming nature of the Christian life, they sidestep the cross and focus primarily on the resurrection. But the cross is the only pathway to an abundant life. No cross no resurrection.

Some churches in Western nations today minimize the cross in their messaging, and here's why. Their concern is that, if they speak of the gruesome aspects of the cross, their gospel will be perceived as morbid and sincere seekers will be repelled.

But Jesus didn't quite seem to see it like that. In speaking of His death, He said, "And I, if I am lifted up from the earth, will draw all peoples to Myself" (John 12:32). He was saying that, when His cross is extolled, He will use it as a magnet to draw all peoples to Himself. The cross is the most compelling attraction of our faith. It has a centripetal gravity all its own. You don't have to defend the cross; just exalt the cross, and it *will* draw people to Christ.

Can You See the Cross?

Nobody who was at the cross actually saw it. Nobody stood before the impaled King, lifted their voice, and cried, "You're the real, authentic Passover Lamb of God. You're purchasing men for God from every tribe and nation. With this sacrifice, You're changing world history. You're fighting the greatest battle of all time. You're making a way for men to draw near to God. Finish Your course! Take courage and fight! We're standing with You!"

They stood and stared at the crucifixion while it was happening, but nobody actually perceived what was going on. Nobody extolled its glory. The only ones who spoke up were those who blasphemed, mocked, and reviled (Mark 15:29-32). It was the biggest event of world history, and yet nobody watching it saw it.

You may experience something similar in your pilgrimage. Sometimes the biggest moments in our lives are unperceived by the people around us.

He's a Lamb to His friends and a Lion to His enemies.

Only two voices came close to speaking something positive over the crucified Savior, and those came from the most unlikely sources. The first was the dying thief who said: "Lord, remember me when You come into Your kingdom" (Luke 23:42). He could probably read the accusation over Jesus' head, *King of the Jews*, and for some reason He believed it. He believed the King dying next to him was going to come into His kingdom, and he verbally expressed his desire to be included. The second voice was that of the centurion overseeing Christ's crucifixion. "So when the centurion, who stood opposite Him, saw that He cried out like this and breathed His last, he said, 'Truly this Man was the Son of God!'" (Mark 15:39). These two are the only voices that expressed something positive about the significance of the moment.

Why couldn't the people staring at Jesus see what was happening? How could they be present at the actual event and yet be so unperceptive? But then I realize, we're hardly any different today. We're looking at the cross still today, *and we don't see it, either.* Why are we still just as dull? Every Easter, millions of people around the world look at the cross without actually seeing it.

Jesus' birth had many prophetic witnesses: angels, shepherds, magi, Anna, Simeon, Elizabeth, Zacharias, and Mary. All of them prophesied about the significance of His coming. But at His death, which voices were prophesying its significance? None.

Sometimes in our lives we experience similar dynamics. When we go to start something, it's not uncommon for people to predict great success in the new endeavor. But later, when we go through the valley of the shadow of death, people will often stare in silence and gape in wonder at our struggle.

Nobody was perceptive enough to stand with Jesus at His trial, scourging, or crucifixion. Nobody spoke up and said, "I'm with Him." Not Peter, not John, not anybody. They couldn't see it.

How about you? Can *you* see it?

Pilate brought Jesus before the crowd and called out, "Behold the Man!" (John19:5). That invitation continues to echo through the centuries. We're invited, when we behold His contorted fingers, to "muse on the work of His hands" (Ps 143:5) and "see the works of God" (Ps 66:5). His bloated, bloody hands were accomplishing a great, historic work—look on it until you can see it.

What Did Bartimaeus See?

I wonder what Bartimaeus saw when he looked at the cross. Yes, I believe Bartimaeus was in the throng at the crucifixion of Christ. Who was he? He was a blind man from Jericho whom Jesus healed on His way to the Passover. When he received his sight, he followed Jesus to Jerusalem (Mark 10:52). I mean, why not? Why not walk in the entourage of the Man who just healed you? Why not see Jerusalem for the first time in your life? Why not participate in your first-ever Passover?

When Bartimaeus arrived with Jesus in Jerusalem, I'm convinced he stayed until Passover. Think about it. Jesus was teaching every morning; the city was buzzing; Passover was only five days away; the atmosphere was electric. He had come this far and now nothing was going to peel him away from witnessing his first Passover.

Nothing, that is, except this—the Man who had healed him just days earlier was now being hauled off to be crucified. The sudden turn of events was startling and overpowering. He was so stunned, he just had to follow the processional to Golgotha.

He watched them pound the nails and hoist the cross. I reckon he had no idea how to process the spectacle his eyes were beholding. His Healer was dying, and he

If you're not distracted by the cross, you're still not seeing it.

couldn't understand it. *Bartimaeus, what did you see?*

That's the beauty of the cross—you don't have to understand it to behold it.

I wonder if Bartimaeus felt cheated or disappointed. I mean, he was excitedly looking forward to seeing his first Passover, but suddenly those plans were hijacked because Jesus of Nazareth was being crucified right in front of him. The Passover was happening in the temple at that very hour, and he was missing it!

But wait a minute. Maybe he didn't miss much after all because, hanging on the middle cross that day was the *ultimate* Passover Lamb. In actuality, Bartimaeus didn't simply see just *any* Passover; he saw *the* Passover—the real, unprecedented, one-of-a-kind, never-to-be-repeated, history-splitting Passover. By standing at Golgotha, his newly-opened eyes didn't miss a thing.

It's Totally Distracting

Like Bartimaeus, are you distracted by the cross? Are the people in your social world distracted by it? Is there even *anyone* in the world today who is distracted by it?

It's the elephant in the room. Everyone at the party is sequestered to their social cliques in various corners of the house, and nobody seems to be acknowledging that there's a huge cross in the middle of the room.

When you finally see and acknowledge the cross, it becomes totally distracting. To introduce any other topic into the conversation seems trivial and trite.

If you're not distracted by the cross, are you even in the room?

It's gripping, arresting, unavoidable, and inescapable. When you see it, you're pulled in by its gravitational vortex. You're transfixed by the spectacle before you. It dominates your horizon; it fills your screen.

When you encounter the cross, you can't push past it. You

can't just go on with your day; it brings you to a full stop. How can you get past the contorted nakedness? Or the wheezing, gasping lungs? Or the fire in His eyes? Or the flame in His heart? You're apprehended by the extravagance and extremity of the spectacle before you.

If you're not distracted by the cross, you're not seeing it. What are we supposed to do with a God who has nails in hands, nails in His feet, a crown of thorns on His head, and lacerations all over His body? What are we supposed to do with a crucified God?

Just a couple days earlier, Philip had asked Jesus, "Show us the Father" (John 14:8). What he probably didn't realize, as he stared at the impaled Savior, was that Jesus was answering his request. Earlier, Jesus had replied to Philip, "He who has seen Me has seen the Father" (John 14:9). Now, in seeing the cruciform Christ, Philip was beholding the Father. The cross was the best way the Father could show Himself to our planet. At the cross, here's what you see about the Father: He's suffering more than anyone can imagine, and He's always laying His life down for everyone. Forever.

When we actually *see* the cross, we just want to worship. We want to give Him everything—all our heart, soul, mind, and strength. We want to lavish our praise upon the Lamb.

Here's the thing about praise: It wants to match the greatness of the accomplishment. For example, when Steve Jobs (mastermind and co-founder of Apple Corporation) died, everyone rose to laud the genius of his accomplishments. Writers and commentators around the world were reaching for language to befit the significance of his legacy. They wanted their praise to properly reflect the impact of his contributions.

In a similar way, when you really see the cross, you reach for praise that rises to the grandeur of Golgotha. Once you've seen the Lamb, you lose interest in holding to your dignity. Now, like David in

Toss your safe, plastic, domesticated image of the cross and behold its shock and scandal.

Psalm 108:1, you want to gather your glory and dignity and prostrate all of it at the nail-scarred feet of Him who gave His all for you. Praise is always searching for expressions commensurate to the magnificence of Calvary.

David wrote, "I will sing and give praise, even with my glory" (Ps 108:1). When he spoke of praising God with his glory, he was referring to all the regal splendor God had given him as the most powerful king on earth. God had crowned him with majesty, honor, dignity, nobility, prestige, supremacy, and authority. Now, in the presence of God's surpassing greatness, David wanted to gather all the glory he had received and empty it on Him by casting it all at His feet. In fact, he explored what it meant to give *undignified praise*. In the presence of the King, he wasn't trying to hold onto his glory, he was trying to empty it on his Lord.

When we really see the cross, we want to do the same. We want to gather all the dignity of who we've become and prostrate it before the Lamb in undignified praise. We want to take the crown we've fought for and cast it before Him who enabled our every achievement. We want a crown—not so we can wear it, but so we have something to throw down. We want our praise to match the unrivaled achievements of the cross.

Are you distracted by the cross? Are you able to see it yet? When you do, you'll lose interest in holding to your dignity. Like the twenty-four elders around the throne, you can't get on your face fast enough. You're floored in the presence of the Lamb.

Lift up the cross! Speak its praises and extol its majesty! "Seven times a day I praise You, because of Your righteous judgments" (Ps 119:164).

For Group Study and Discussion

1. How can we give stronger visibility to the cross in our churches?

2. *The cross is our message for the world*: Do you agree? Why or why not?

3. In what ways does the cross draw people to Jesus? (John 12:32)

4. Can you think of any topics that we don't usually see the cross as addressing, but would come into focus if we could just see the cross?

5. When you imagine "blind Bartimaeus" looking at the cross, what might have been going on in his heart?

6. *The cross is the elephant in the room*: What are the implications of that idea?

7. As you close your group time, choose a verse from this chapter to pray. Pray it over each person in the group.

CHAPTER FIVE

Metaphors for the Cross

As already stated, the cross is our calibrator, center, and crux. These metaphors help us visualize and cherish its depth of meaning. In this chapter, I want to explore even more metaphors that help us appreciate the wonders of the cross.

What is a metaphor? *A figure of speech in which a word is applied to an object to which it is not literally applicable.* May the following metaphors make the wisdom of the cross even more glorious and understandable for you.

The Cross Is a Lens

Glasses have a pair of lenses that help the user see objects more clearly. In a similar way, the cross is a lens that helps bring all of life into better focus. God wanted the cross to be our lens from the very beginning, but we struggled to perceive it. When Jesus was hanging on the cross, the Father was finally able to point and say, *This is what I've been saying to you all along. Now can you see what I mean?* At the cross, the Father's heart became clear, and now we're able to see the way of salvation and the way of sacrificial servanthood.

The Scriptures come into better focus when viewed through the lens of the cross. Some verses explode with fresh meaning when interpreted in light of Calvary. Name the biblical issue, and the cross will help us see it better.

Someone once said that all truth is God's truth. View all truth everywhere, therefore, through the lens of the cross. This applies to every educational course you take, no matter the school. Truth is found in many scholastic disciplines, but so is falsehood. How can we distinguish between them, keep the true, and discard the false? By subjecting every propositional statement to the scrutiny of the cross. View every lecture and textbook through the lens of the cross, and you'll become skillful in preserving truth and detecting error.

When you hang with your friends, you probably chat sometimes about the values of your culture—such as justice, equality, liberty, compassion, identity, etc. Opinions on these topics abound, and discerning what is true can be challenging. If you evaluate every opinion through the lens of the cross, however, you'll be equipped to recognize truth and resist the twisted thinking of the world. The cross will help you understand how to respond to injustices perpetrated by people against you or others. For example, when talking about the hot-button topic of racial tensions, the way forward gets clearer when we bring the discussion to the foot of the cross. The cross calls us to lose our lives and lay them down for people of all skin colors and languages. We find the world's narrative on issues such as racism inadequate because they don't surrender their perspectives to the wisdom of the cross.

When people try to help you find your life and save your life, you'll have the discernment to see your circumstances through a lens they can't see. The cross will keep you from "walking in the counsel of the ungodly" (Ps 1:1).

As you process current events through the lens of the cross, the Lord will open your eyes to His perspective on world events.

Interpret every voice you hear and every line you read through the lens of the cross, and you'll be able to make judgments and decisions that accord with light, truth, wisdom, and understanding.

Make the cross your lens.

The Cross Is Our Balance Beam

The cross is the balance beam of Christianity. What is a balance beam? It's a horizontal beam of wood upon which

| Impossible to make the cross too large. |

gymnasts perform impressive feats of strength and agility, all the while maintaining their equilibrium on the narrow bar. Like that beam, the cross is our point of reference that enables us to maintain a balanced stance in all areas of truth and practice. It keeps our theology calibrated and aligned.

Every excessive and weird doctrine has strayed from the centrality of the cross. The cross safeguards us from imbalanced ideas and helps us weed out false teachings before they spread in the church. If you come across a novel teaching that you're not sure about, measure it against the plumb line of the cross. Does it line up? Does it honor and support everything the cross represents? If you use the cross to maintain your theological balance, you'll be preserved in truth.

Many of my friends have told me they see the *resurrection* as the central pillar of our faith, and the cross as the necessary lead-in or prelude to that great, central event. I love their passion for the resurrection because I share it, and their preference here is not bad or wrong. But for me, the *cross* is the central pillar, and the resurrection the natural outcome or consequence of that great event.

When the churches of Galatia got imbalanced and strayed into doctrinal error, Paul wrote the book of Galatians—something like a balance beam—to get them centered again on the true gospel. Not once in that book did he mention the resurrection, but he mentioned the cross seven times (Gal 2:20; 3:1, 13; 5:11, 24; 6:12, 14), and nine times if you include two secondary references (2:21; 6:17). When calling them to get centered again in the gospel, he didn't use the resurrection as his basis of appeal. He used the cross! It's our balance beam.

When various groups stray into imbalanced doctrine, examine their emphasis closely and you'll likely find that, while they still trumpet the resurrection of Christ, they grow quietly distant in their emphasis of the cross. When we get quiet about the cross, we lose our balance.

Use the cross to challenge imbalanced ideas. When you're

in a room where ideas are being discussed or debated, the cross defogs the room. Like a noise cancellation feature on a set of headphones, it silences the noise and muffles the chatter. Bring the cross into the discussion and you may be stunned at the way it silences the cacophony and brings clarity to the issues at hand.

I never feel safer than when clinging to the cross. It maintains my equilibrium. If I can't get something through the cross, I'm not taking it with me.

The Cross Is an Anchor

The cross is the anchor of our faith. The writer of Hebrews portrayed our hope in Christ as an anchor that's tethered to the mercy seat in heaven where Christ has sprinkled His blood (Heb 6:19-20). When we're anchored to this heavenly rock, nothing on earth can shipwreck us.

The cross anchors our faith in the midst of life's storms. Storms come equally to the wise and foolish (Matt 7:24-27), but here's what distinguishes the wise: They survive the storm. Why? Because they're anchored. Just as an anchor helps a boat survive a tempest, the cross will anchor your faith and enable you to weather life's storms. When you're anchored by the cross, you can come through a storm even better for it.

Storms come in many shapes and sizes, and they often shake our faith. When it feels like everything in your life is being shaken, take some advice from this pilgrim and return to the cross. It can't be shaken, and clinging to it will save you.

I wish I could say to every young person going through a faith crisis: *Go back to the cross.* Are you disoriented by a swirl of questions? Go back to the cross. Does it seem like God is distant and silent to your prayers? Go back to the cross. Gaze again at His bloodied hands and feet. When nothing

The wisdom of the cross arrests arguments and clears foggy thinking.

else can hold your heart, the cross will. It's strong enough to anchor your heart in any storm.

I have both arms and legs wrapped around the cross of Christ. I've decided that, if it goes down, I'm going down with it.

The Cross Is Our GPS

A GPS (Global Positioning System) device uses satellite signals to help us navigate toward a destination. In a similar way, the cross uses Holy Spirit signals to direct our steps in the way of righteousness. When we wonder, "How do I get from here to there?" the cross shows the way: *Walk the Via Dolorosa.*

How do I make a lasting difference in my world?" *By losing your life.*

The greatest race ever run was won by a Man whose feet were nailed to a tree. From that tree, He's showing you how to run your race, too.

The wisdom of the cross will show you how to live life skillfully. Follow the bloody trail of His feet and you'll eventually make it to your eternal destination.

The Cross Is a Dipstick

God used the cross like a dipstick to show us His love for the world. Someone might ask, "What's a dipstick?" It's a narrow strip of metal that mechanics thrust into the engine block of a car to measure its oil level. In a similar way, the Father took the cross, thrust it into the blood of Calvary, showed its measurements to the world, and said, "This is how much I love you."

Furthermore, the cross also measures *us.* Using the cross like a dipstick, the Father evaluates the hearts and souls of men and women. He plunges it below every façade and reveals what's really happening on the inside.

The cross locates us and confronts us with the true condition of our hardened hearts. You really can't look at the naked Christ without being denuded yourself. At first glance, when looking upon the crucified Savior—hung before the gaping gaze of a crowd of spectators—you're struck with how exposed He is. But then you realize, He wasn't the only one on Golgotha laid bare that day; *everyone* at the cross was being exposed and measured.

Simeon had prophesied about it years earlier when he said, "The thoughts of many hearts will be revealed" (Luke 2:35). And sure enough, at the cross *everyone's* thoughts were revealed—priests, soldiers, Pilate, dying thieves, and the entire gallery of witnesses. You couldn't watch without it measuring and revealing you.

This dipstick is still measuring all of us today.

Actually, the cross is a metric against which almost *anything* can be assessed. You can use it, like a dipstick, to evaluate circumstances, situations, and current cultural issues. I recommend examining *everything* according to its height and length.

The Cross Is Our Emblem

The cross is the emblem of our faith.

Someone once suggested to me, "I don't think the cross should be the emblem of our faith but rather the empty tomb. If we're going to put something around our neck, it shouldn't be a cross but an empty tomb."

I appreciate that person's sincerity and zeal for the resurrection of Christ, but I actually disagree with that opinion. I'm persuaded the cross *is* the emblem of Christianity, and here's why. The compelling distinctive of our faith is not that God is alive—*many* religions and faiths believe that. The compelling distinctive of our faith is that God died.

That God should resurrect from the

> The way to the Father is as narrow as the wood on which Jesus was crucified.

chains of hell with everlasting life coursing through His being doesn't astonish us; what stuns us is that Eternal Life died. The death of God is the part of the story that's utterly astounding!

Where did this idea come from? Who came up with the idea of God suffering a hideously grotesque death? This notion is so preposterous and scandalous that no human mind conceived it. This didn't originate on earth but descended from heaven.

What other religion brags on the death of its leader?

The Cross Is Our Coat of Arms

A coat of arms is *a crest, badge of heraldry, or shield of family, corporation, or country.* The cross, therefore, is our banner, shield, and ensign. It's our coat of arms—the insignia of our loyalty to the Lamb.

The cross is all about loyalty. First of all, it reveals the loyalty of Jesus to His Father. He didn't want to do the cross, but He did it anyway out of fierce loyalty to His Father's will. Even when Abba forsook Him (Matt 27:46), He remained loyal— unto death. Therefore, it's the ultimate act of loyalty.

Secondly, the cross inspires our loyalty to Jesus. Anyone that loyal to the Father deserves all my fealty. Clutching it to my breast, once again I swear my head to the cross of Jesus Christ. He died for me and I'll willingly die for Him. I proudly parade this coat of arms every day as I walk out into the world. As goes the old hymn, "Onward, Christian soldiers, marching as to war."[1]

When "the evil day" of Ephesians 6:13 or "the hour of trial" of Revelation 3:10 comes your way, your loyalty will be tested. Only one thing is strong enough to hold your heart in that hour. I advise you, therefore, to fasten your heart around the cross *now* so that its holding power will carry you *then.* When they come to torture and kill you, it'll seal your resolve

---

1   Sabine Baring-Gould, 1864.

and set your face as flint. Hold it close to your heart and let it always be your coat of arms.

Judge the Cross

You can't dismiss the cross; you must judge the cross. When confronted with it, no one can remain neutral. What is it—*really*? What verdict will you render?

In reality, there are only two options. Either it's the greatest hoax of history that deserves to be trampled, reviled, and spat upon, or it's the greatest hope of human history—something worth dying for.

Hoax or heroic—which is it? You be the judge.

Our answer has a direct bearing on our judgment regarding hell. Before you make a determination about whether you think hell is real or not, you must first make a determination regarding the cross. Here's why.

If there is no hell, the cross is absurd. The cross makes sense only if it's saving us from something utterly hellish.

If you decide the cross is a hoax, then I suppose you can dismiss the existence of hell and be on your way. But if you judge the cross to be the heroic intervention of God, its extremity points to the extremity of the hell from which we're saved.

> The Carpenter crafted His greatest work with the wood of a cross.

For Group Study and Discussion

1. Read Mark 14-16 this week, and share with the group what moved you most in this reading of the crucifixion account.

2. The cross is a lens, balance beam, anchor, GPS, dipstick, emblem, and coat of arms. Which metaphor did you enjoy the most, and why?

3. Read the book of Galatians this week, ponder all the places where Paul referred to the cross, and bring your observations to the group discussion.

4. In what ways does the cross anchor our faith?

5. How can we invite our unbelieving friends to behold and judge the cross? (as hoax or heroic)

6. *If there is no hell, the cross is absurd*: Talk about that statement. How does the cross inform our understanding of hell?

7. As you close your group time, center your prayers around Galatians 2:20.

CHAPTER SIX

Dangerous Love

With arms nailed wide open to you, the cross was Jesus' most articulate way to say, "I love you." He didn't love you with 99 percent of His heart but with His entire being. Death didn't take His life. Love did.

Anything for love!

He found a hill with a garden in it so that He could propose. With nails in His hands, nails in His feet, and a spear protruding from His side, He says, "Marry Me. Give Me your everything and I'll give you Mine."

To define love, don't search online, but look instead to the cross. Ira F. Stanphill said it this way in his hymn: "He wrote His love in crimson red."[2]

Jesus, mark me with this love. Take a nail, dip it in blood, and write Your name on my heart.

A Violent Torrent

We had a pretty nice religion there for a while, until the cross came along. It changed everything. It ripped the innards out. Like a bursting dam, the cross inundated our planet with a deluge of divine love. It came through like a tsunami and swept the place clean of propriety and dignity and modesty. You can't even have your clothes.

The cross is a violent torrent of love. It's dangerous, all-consuming, and demanding of everything. Now, nothing is safe. Love came along like a torrential river, caught Christ in its rushing rapids, and carried Him to His death. If that same current of love grabs hold of your legs, it will sweep *you* off your feet, too, and carry you to *your* death. But losing your life you'll find it.

Jesus didn't go around saying to people, "I love you." It wasn't His style.

> The greatest battle ever fought was won by a Man who just stood on the nail.

He didn't go around *telling* people He loved them; He went around *showing* people He loved them. I'm not sure, therefore, that we should go around *telling* the world we love them; instead, we should go around *showing* the world we love them.

Jesus showed me His love on the cross, and O what a love I saw! I denied Him, betrayed Him, tried Him, delivered Him to Pilate, scourged Him, beat Him, spat on Him, crowned Him with thorns, pounded nails into His hands and feet, mocked Him, and thrust a spear in His side. And here's what He did back: He washed me, changed my name, gave me the best robe, put a ring on my finger, sandals on my feet, sat me at the table, and gave me the family fortune.

What kind of love is this?

I drew His blood and then He washed me with it. Little wonder I love Him so! What else can be said except—*Worthy is the Lamb to receive all power, riches, wisdom, strength, honor, glory, majesty, dominion, blessing, praise, thanksgiving, and adoration!*

An Inferno

The cross is a raging flame—kindled by the fiery love Jesus has for us. It's a fiery exchange in which He loves us and we love Him with the same flaming passions. He loves first, enabling us to love Him in return with God-sized affections. It's all about blazing love.

When you see how painful the cross was, you realize how passionately He feels about you—which is why He spews the lukewarm from His mouth (Rev 3:16). He didn't take it in His hands and feet to get a bride who yawns in His face on Sunday mornings. He died for a bride who feels as deeply about Him as He feels about her, who has a fire in her heart like He has in His, who looks at Him the way He looks at her, and who is as loyal to His cross as He is to hers.

When I think of the cross's flaming love, I'm reminded of this proverb:

> There are three things that are never satisfied, four never say, "Enough!": The grave, the barren womb, the earth that is not satisfied with water—and the fire never says, "Enough!" (Prov 30:15-16).

The fire never says, "Enough." Just as natural flames never abate from being satisfied, the fire of Christ's love is unrelenting in its desire for more. When that love kindles us and makes us firebrands of love, we're also filled with a love that's never exhausted and that never says, "Enough."

The fire of God's love in our hearts always wants more. We want to be closer to Him, to see His beauty more clearly, to feel His presence more tangibly, and to receive more of His power and life. Never enough love! Our love always reaches out, "More, Lord! I want more!"

God's burning heart responds, "Me too. I want more, too." Whenever we go, "I want more of You, Lord," He responds, "And I want more of you."

This is the romance of the cross—where we're both giving and receiving more and more love. The whole journey is a romantic adventure, exploring the question, *How can I give more?* We're not asking, *How little can I get away with giving?* but, *How can I give Him even more?*

This is the extravagant, fiery love of the cross.

Why So Intense?

We look at the cross and wonder, why is the suffering so extreme? I see at least five reasons:

1. The cross was so intense to reveal how *dark* sin really is. The cross was so dreadfully stark because sin is so dreadfully dark. God wants us to see sin for what it truly is—exceedingly sinful (Rom 7:13).

> On the cross, He didn't *demand* our love but *won* our love.

2. The cross was so intense to reveal the incredible value of humanity. The value of something is determined by the price someone is willing to pay for it. Look at the price God paid for us! Psalm 49:8 was certainly true, "The redemption of their souls is costly." The cost of Calvary discloses just how precious we are in His sight. As a wise merchant, Jesus looked at the pearl He would gain in His bride and said, "It's worth it. I'll pay the price." Our value in His eyes is beyond calculation.

3. The cross was so intense to demonstrate the extravagance of God's love for us. This is the message of the often-quoted verse, John 3:16. The cross demonstrates the #CrazyLove the Father has for us.

4. The cross was so intense to establish beyond all argument that the price for our salvation was paid in full. Satan always complains at the way God honors His children, accusing Him of using undeserving vessels and using His power to unfair advantage (Zech 3). But after Calvary, Satan is rendered speechless at how God uses it because Calvary was extravagant overpayment.

5. The cross was so intense to reveal the strength of our mighty Champion who violently took the kingdom of heaven by force (Matt 11:12). At the cross, you're not looking at how violent people can be against God, but how violent God can be against an enemy. He took the violent measures necessary to strongarm our salvation.

The Wicked Made Righteous

The crucifixion of Christ was the greatest injustice of human history. Had justice been served Him, He would have been honored and revered by His generation as the wisest, kindest, and most benevolent Teacher of all time. Instead,

He was killed as though He were a villain. Pilate's decision to crucify Jesus was the grossest injustice ever perpetrated by a human court.

If there's anything that's important to God, it's *justice* (Isa 61:8). God's fierce sense of justice demands that injustice be answered. God couldn't just wink at the thing and let it go. No! Such a gross injustice *had* to be answered and justice upheld.

Furthermore, the injustice of the cross was so monolithic that its satisfaction had to be equally massive and historic. How would God rectify the injustice of the cross? Would He fry the whole planet to a crisp? No, destroying the earth would be an insufficient answer. He had to do something even more drastic.

What God did, to answer the injustice of the cross, is so dumbfounding that it's almost offensive. To Satan, it's an absurd injustice all its own. *God used the injustice of the cross to render malicious sinners altogether just in His presence (when they repent).* The cross gave God the legal capital He needed to do the preposterous: make willful sinners just.

God was like, "There's only one thing that will answer an injustice as horrific as the cross. Whenever a vile sinner takes the cross on their lips by faith, they must be rendered righteous." Only grace could satisfy such a grievous injustice in such a remarkable way!

God's salvation is so extreme it's stunning. It's borderline raucous, borderline sacrilegious, borderline reckless, borderline absurd. He now makes the unrighteous righteous—without compromising His own righteousness (see Rom 3:26). When wicked sinners are made completely righteous by faith, then the injustice of the cross is finally and fully satisfied. Who ever thought of such a thing? A God who is mighty to save and strong to deliver!

Yes, *this* is how God loves the world.

We're in a blood covenant with Jesus Christ. He supplied the blood.

No Killing this Love

I see the personal nature of Christ's love for us in the Lord's Supper. When Jesus instituted that Supper, He said, "This is My body, and this is My blood. Here, eat and drink." And then He Himself served the bread and cup. Every time we receive Communion, Jesus still serves the meal. He takes a piece of His broken body and gives it to us. Then, He gathers some of His spilled blood and hands it to us. The thing that makes the meal so incredibly intimate is the way He personally gives us His own body and blood.

The cross searched, explored, and excavated God's love. It seemed to test and assess the limits of His love. It seemed to explore questions such as, *Could love survive the cross, or would it collapse? In this great showdown between love and death, could love be conquered by death? Could love drink the whole cup without crumbling?*

The cross proved that God's love is stronger than death. Scripture had described God's love as *unfailing* and *everlasting* (Lam 3:22; Jer 31:3), and now it was proven so. Not even death could extinguish this everlasting love.

If death can't kill God's love, what can? *Nothing.* Nothing is "able to separate us from the love of God which is in Christ Jesus our Lord" (Rom 8:39). His love never fails!

For Group Study and Discussion

1. Viewing the cross as a statement of love, which sentence in this chapter stood out to you the most, and why?

2. Talk about the violent, dangerous love of the cross. What does this mean for your life?

3. *He didn't take it in His hands and feet to get a bride who yawns in His face on Sunday mornings.* What do you think about that statement?

4. Of the five reasons given for why the cross was so intense, which one grabbed your attention most? Can you think of any other reasons?

5. Talk about the paradox between Proverbs 17:15 and Romans 4:5. How does this help you appreciate the cross?

6. How does the Lord's Supper help you connect with the cross?

7. As you close your group time, would you want to receive Communion together? Center your prayers around John 3:16.

CHAPTER SEVEN
A Collaborative Effort

At Calvary's construction site, all three Persons of the Trinity were present and working collaboratively to procure our salvation. The cross was such a massive undertaking that it took the entire Godhead to pull it off.

What was the Father doing at Golgotha? He was loving the world by pouring out a cup—the cup of His wrath against sin. He was expending the entirety of His wrath upon His Son. Tipping the cup, He emptied its contents. And then, when His Son was crying out to Him, He turned His face away and forsook Him—because of the magnitude of His loving plan to redeem us. That's what the Father was doing.

What was the Son doing at the cross? He was drinking the cup (Matt 26:42). He stood on the nail, opened up, took the Father's cup of sorrows, and drained it to the bottom.

What was the Holy Spirit doing at the cross? He too was working, but here's where the scriptural record is somewhat sparing. In what manner was the Holy Spirit laboring during the crucifixion? We're not told much, but we get a glimpse in Hebrews 9:14, "Christ...through the eternal Spirit offered Himself without spot to God." The Holy Spirit was helping Jesus die.

After all, Jesus dubbed Him *the Helper* (John 14:26). That's because He helps. He can't help Himself, it's just what He does. He's always helping everyone who asks, everywhere, all the time. As the Helper, He helped Jesus complete His assignment on the cross and offer Himself without sin to God.

Is it possible—and I'm speaking now in the limitations of my human understanding—there came a time, during the course of the crucifixion, when the Father asked within Himself, *How can I continue to do this? How can I continue to expend My wrath against sin upon My Son in whom I'm so well pleased?* I wonder if the Holy Spirit came alongside and whispered, *You can do it. You can empty the cup in its entirety. I will help You.*

Is it possible—and I'm speaking again in the limitations of my human understanding—there came a time during those lonely hours on Golgotha when the Son asked within Himself, *How can I continue to do this? How can I continue to drink this cup the Father is giving Me?* If there had been such a moment, I wonder if the Holy Spirit came alongside and whispered, *You can do it. You can finish off the whole thing. I will help You.*

Yes, the cross was such an enormous endeavor that it required the reserves of the entire Trinity to pull it off. It was God using all His strength to come to our rescue.

Some people struggle with the idea that the Father crucified Jesus. The suffering is so extreme that they can't imagine the Father its perpetrator. For example, I once heard a preacher say he was offended at the suggestion that the Father killed Jesus at Calvary. But since Paul wrote about "the offense of the cross," I suppose we shouldn't be too surprised when it offends (Gal 5:11; 1 Cor 1:23). But don't imagine the Father insulated from Jesus' sufferings. At the cross, the entire Godhead suffered to accomplish this salvation. It was both collaborative exertion and collaborative suffering.

Not only did the Father crucify Jesus, but He did so cheerfully. He "loves a cheerful giver" (2 Cor 9:7) because He is one. At the cross, the Father gave Jesus to us, not under compulsion but cheerfully. Isaiah 53:10 said it *pleased* the Father to bruise Him. But wasn't the Father also distraught? Yes. That God was both distraught and cheerful at the cross testifies to His immense capacity for love.

How did the Son feel about His Father cheerfully giving Him up to crucifixion? Look to Psalm 18:35 for an answer: "Your gentleness has made Me great." Jesus called His Father's cup *gentleness*. How could Jesus cast the extreme torments of the cross as

> If God can do a thousand years' work in one day at the cross (2 Pet 3:8), He can do a lifetime work in you in a moment of time.

gentleness? Because it was the Father's gentlest option for redeeming a fallen world. I suppose Jesus thinking, *Their sin is so terribly dark, Abba, that at the cross You were actually gentle with Me in atoning for their sin. And now look—Your gentleness has made Me great.*

At the crucifixion, we wondered, "What kind of Father are You, anyway?" At the resurrection, we got our answer. "You're magnificently benevolent, gentle, and generous!" The dangerous love of the cross opened to the most magnificent glory imaginable. As Arthur Katz once said, the cross is the most perfect theological statement of who God is.

Jesus' Love for His Father

The cross displayed the flaming love that burns within the Trinity. At the cross, love was expressed in at least three ways. First of all, it showed the love that Jesus has for His Father.

Jesus didn't want to do the cross because, like anyone in a human body, He didn't want to suffer. He did it only because He loved His Father so much. He deferred to His Father's will and died in absolute loyalty. The cross was Jesus saying to the Father, "I love You. I'll do anything for You."

We see Jesus' love for His Father in the way He fixated upon Him during the crucifixion. During those six hours, He kept looking at His Father and talking to Him. For example, of His seven sayings on the cross, four of them—the majority—were spoken to His Father. It's as though He was saying, "Abba, I have eyes only for You." We're not told in Scripture how the Father might have talked back to Him, but I can imagine the Father responding in the language of Song 6:5, "Turn Your eyes away from Me, for they have overcome Me." And I can imagine Jesus responding, "Where else shall I look? You're My only one, My life, My source, My sanity, My survival. You fill My horizon. You're all I see."

Yes, the cross was Jesus demonstrating His love for the Father.

God's Love for the World

Secondly, the cross showed us the Father's love for the world. Exactly how does the Father love the world? The answer is supplied at the cross where, out of love for the world, "He gave His only begotten Son" (John 3:16). The cross demonstrated how lavishly He loves every person in the world—of every ethnicity, economic strata, nation, skin color, age, and gender. He loves every enemy and every rebel, regardless of how deeply they've drunk of sin. The Father of creation yearns and longs for all His children, especially those estranged from Him. He loves them so much He sacrificed His favorite Son.

This is the love that the cross emanates to the world.

Christ's Love for Us

Thirdly, the cross revealed Christ's love for us. When John wrote, "To Him who loved us and washed us from our sins in His own blood" (Rev 1:5), he was saying that Jesus, in the shedding of His blood, was loving us. We're meant to look at the cross and see just how much He loves us.

We weren't satisfied with just killing Him; we wanted to torment Him on His way out. Therefore, we hammered on His raw nerve endings, blow upon blow, to inflict maximum pain. And how did He respond? By loving us! As Paul said, He "loved me and gave Himself for me" (Gal 2:20).

His love for you is so strong it killed Him. He died just for you, and He means for you to take it personally.

To understand the extremity of Christ's love, consider how Paul embodied it. Paul embodied the love of the cross in a way that's both compelling and practical. We'll see it by comparing Romans 8 with Romans 9. When you see this, you'll see how Jesus loved us on the cross.

In Romans 8, Paul wrote one of the most glorious litanies on the love of God

> Not even the resurrection showed the limits of God's power. Nobody knows how strong He really is.

in all Scripture. He said nothing can separate us from God's love and, if anything tries, it only sets us up to be more than conquerors through Him who loved us. Death, life, angels, principalities, powers, things present, things to come, height, depth, anything created—*none* of these things are "able to separate us from the love of God which is in Christ Jesus our Lord" (Rom 8:39).

Moving into the next chapter, Paul described what happened in him when God filled him with His love. God's love for him placed within him a profound love for his fellow countrymen. He expressed it this way: "For I could wish that I myself were accursed from Christ for my brethren, my countrymen according to the flesh" (Rom 9:3). Paul was so swept up by God's love that he loved his fellow countrymen with a startling kind of love—*wishing himself damned to hell for eternity if it could mean their salvation.*

Wow! Romans 8 love for God had given Paul Romans 9 love for his countrymen.

Paul had received this love from the cross. Therefore, I believe Jesus had the same sentiment in His heart on the cross. I believe Jesus was thinking, *Abba, I wish that I could be accursed from You forever, if it could mean the salvation of every man and woman You've created.* Such an arrangement was impossible because salvation requires that people exercise faith; but still, this was the kind of love Jesus embodied on the cross. Jesus loves the human race so much He wished He could do hell forever in our place. Since that wasn't possible, He did the next closest thing—the cross. When this love won Paul's heart, it gripped him with the same extravagant love for his fellow countrymen. In love, Paul labored to lose his life so others could be saved.

When the love of the cross captures our hearts, we too could wish ourselves accursed from Christ forever if it could mean the salvation of our fellow countrymen. This is how much Christ loves us, and now this is how much we love our neighbor!

Love's Dimensions

The limits of Christ's love are inexhaustible and surpass knowledge. Paul wrote about it with these sublime words:

> That you, being rooted and grounded in love, may be able to comprehend with all the saints what is the width and length and depth and height—to know the love of Christ which passes knowledge; that you may be filled with all the fullness of God (Eph 3:17-19).

Paul described Christ's love as extending in four directions: high, low, wide, and deep. The cross illustrates all four. And there's no end to the scope of each, making each of these four a veritable *universe* of love to be explored. Look at the four directions the love of the cross reaches.

The horizontal stipe of the cross signifies the *width* of God's love. With arms nailed open on the horizontal post, His hands point outward to show His love reaching from horizon to horizon. The spread of His arms seems to say, "This is how much I love you." The nails seem to be His friends as they help Him spread His hands further. His love is wide enough to encompass every continent, nation, people group, island, tribe, language, and ethnicity, embracing *everyone*.

The downward post of the cross, where His feet are impaled, points to the *length* of God's love. His love goes down, down, down to the lowest pit. It descends to the invisible cell of the mentally tormented; to the darkest, foulest prison; to the caged prostitute; to the homeless alcoholic's hovel; to the serial killer; to the torture chamber.

How low can humanity go? The cross goes lower, reaching the deepest dregs of society. You can't go lower than the cross. Jesus sank lower than the most contemptible human being so He could lift us into His family. The cross reaches below the lowest human specimen and, like a giant dipper, lifts them into the

He came to the earth He owned and, rather than insisting on His ownership, paid the full purchase price all over again.

glorious inheritance of the sons of God.

This is why the cross makes our gospel universally relevant. Herein lies its wisdom, for you can take this message anywhere. Try it—take the message of the cross to the worst hellhole on the planet. Find the most destitute, sin-scarred, addiction-bound, demon-possessed, filthy derelict—and you have found someone whom this gospel takes up in its arms. Why? Because the One who suffered on the tree sank lower than all that He might raise up the foulest of sinners and seat them at His table in regal splendor. To what lengths the cross reaches!

Thirdly, the cross demonstrates the *depth* of God's love. I see this aspect of love in His pierced side, where the spear protrudes from His chest cavity. It's almost as though that wound opened a way for us to peer into the cavernous depths of the love that's in His heart. Eternity will not be long enough to exhaust and explore the depths of this love.

Fourthly, the upward post of the cross points to the *height* of God's love. This part of the cross hosted His thorn-crowned head, and it points upward to a vast universe of love that extends above the cross. This love rises to the heavens. It is lofty, noble, majestic, glorious, and sublime. When this love captures and lifts you into the heavenlies, it will dizzy you with its noble supremacy. O the ineffable *heights* of the transcendent love of Christ!

Just like the cross, this love is *wide, long, deep,* and *high.*

The cross stretches *us* to reach out in love in all four directions, too. We need help to love like this, however, because we lack the strength in ourselves to express such boundless love. As the saying goes, *it takes God to love God*—that is, we depend on His love to empower our love.

Come to the cross now, and offer your prayer. Express your desire to receive His love—the width, length, depth, and height of His love. And then ask Him to help you to love in the same way—wide, long, deep, and high.

Jesus, fill me with the love of Your cross!

For Group Study and Discussion

1. Talk about the Holy Spirit's role at the crucifixion. Share your insights on Hebrews 9:14.

2. In love, the Father engineered Christ's crucifixion. Is this difficult for anyone in your group to accept? Can we help each other to understand?

3. Talk about the love the Father and Son share for each other. What other verse provides insight into this love?

4. The Romans 8 love of God gave Paul Romans 9:3 love for his fellow countrymen. How can we love like Romans 9:3?

5. The love of the cross is wide, high, low, and deep. Which of these four fascinates you most?

6. As you close your group time, center your prayers around Ephesians 3:17-19.

CHAPTER EIGHT

Peter and Judas

Peter and Judas Iscariot were both in Jesus' inner circle of twelve disciples, and both had a high profile in the events surrounding the crucifixion. By comparing their participation, we can see how the cross revealed the nature of their love.

In the events surrounding Jesus' arrest and trial, both Peter and Judas failed miserably, but the difference in their failures was very significant. One was restored, and the other lost. The one who was restored—Peter—lost faith, but Judas lost love. Let me explain the difference by starting with Peter.

Peter Lost Faith

At Christ's arrest, Peter had a faith crisis. But it was no surprise to Jesus because He had actually predicted it:

> And the Lord said, "Simon, Simon! Indeed, Satan has asked for you, that he may sift you as wheat. But I have prayed for you, that your faith should not fail; and when you have returned to Me, strengthen your brethren" (Luke 22:31-32).

Peter's faith didn't utterly fail, but it did collapse. He lost faith that he would ultimately win if he stayed at Jesus' side. Suddenly, it appeared that Jesus was losing, and in the uncertainty of the moment, Peter bailed. The intensity of the moment revealed that his faith wasn't as strong as he thought.

How do we know his faith collapsed? Well, he abandoned Jesus at His arrest and fled; and then, during the course of Jesus' trial, Peter denied three times that he knew Him. Just that evening, Jesus had predicted to Peter that he would deny Him three times. Even after Peter realized he had fulfilled the prediction, he couldn't gather his courage and recant his denial. He lacked the faith and courage, in that critical moment, to turn around, walk into the center of the court's proceedings, and stand with Jesus. He still loved, which is why he wept so bitterly, but his faith had collapsed.

Peter Was Sifted

In Jesus' words, Satan sifted him. Satan sifted all the disciples, but he went after the top leader first. Peter's sifting had some elements similar to that of Job's. Here are five observations about Satan's sifting as seen in the book of Job and Luke 22 above:

1. Satan had to ask permission to sift Peter and Job. He can't sift the godly without first soliciting God's permission. God has a wall of protection around His elect that Satan can't penetrate without divine permission.

2. Sometimes God says *yes*. He doesn't give Satan permission every time because God knows the strength and calling of each of His servants. In fact, it seems that God says *no* to Satan more often than not. But occasionally God will give Satan the access he desires.

3. Both Satan and God have their own agenda in the sifting. Satan's agenda is to turn God's servant into a spiritual casualty; God's purpose is to form His servant into an even more effective vessel for the kingdom.

4. When being sifted, you've got Jesus praying for you. Just as Jesus assured Peter that He would pray him through, He'll pray you through, too.

5. When you return to Jesus in renewed faith, you'll strengthen your brethren. It's not the strong but the sifted who strengthen others. The strong might impress or overpower others, but the sifted gain valuable experience in their journey that enable them, in turn, to strengthen others.

Both Job and Peter are dynamic examples of people who were sifted by Satan and came through a better person for it.

Let the cross nail you to the will of God.

Judas Lost Love

In contrast to Peter who lost *faith*, Judas Iscariot lost his *love* for Jesus. His was more a love crisis than a faith crisis. Let's talk about it.

As one of the twelve, Judas was struggling to belong. Peter, James, and John were in Jesus' inner circle, but Judas felt like he was on the periphery. Even though he managed the ministry's finances, he struggled to feel approved by Jesus. The final straw took place during a special dinner in Bethany, during which Mary anointed Jesus with very costly oil of spikenard.

Wanting to impress with his zeal for the poor, Judas spoke up, "Why was this fragrant oil not sold for three hundred denarii and given to the poor?" (John 12:5). Jesus immediately rebuked him, "Let her alone; she has kept this for the day of My burial. For the poor you have with you always, but Me you do not have always" (John 12:7-8). Judas had reproached Mary publicly, so it was appropriate that his rebuke be administered publicly. But it really stung.

It seems Jesus' rebuke changed Judas's outlook on his life. His thinking was quite possibly along the lines of, *Clearly, I don't have a future with Jesus. I believe He's a great Man, but there's no place of advancement for me on the team. I'm always going to be low man on the totem pole. I don't see a way to have the kind of friendship and favor with Him that I've been hoping for. It's time to get in reality, leave the team, and get on with life.*

Judas didn't love Jesus, he loved himself. His passion was not to advance Jesus' cause but his own welfare and career. Jesus' rebuke helped Judas realize he no longer loved the Master.

Why the Betrayal?

For centuries, Christians have wondered why Judas betrayed Jesus for thirty pieces of silver. For me, the evidence suggests he thought he was doing both himself and Jesus a favor. I suppose Judas thinking, *Since I'm leaving the team anyway, I may as well do it in a way that gives both Jesus and me the best advantage. This can be a win-win for both of us.* The money would help secure his own future, and the betrayal would help prod Jesus to show Himself to the world. Jesus would escape arrest, as He always had, and would probably go public with His intentions.

I think one reason Judas kissed Jesus was because he thought he was doing Him a favor: *I'm going to help You make Your move. I'm setting up the scenario You need to really show them who You are. You may not appreciate this right now, but I'm actually being a friend. One day You're going to thank me for this.*

This was the kind of thinking going on in the brethren described in Isaiah 66:5, "Your brethren who hated you, who cast you out for My name's sake, said, 'Let the LORD be glorified, that we may see your joy.' But they shall be ashamed." Isaiah said the brethren were saying to their brother, "We're squeezing you out for your own good, and one day you'll be glad we did." But the Holy Spirit testified, "It's because they hate you." In a similar way, Judas betrayed Jesus because he hated—he had lost his love. He probably still had some faith in Jesus, but no more love.

If you lose your faith, Jesus can pray you through. But if you lose your love, what can be done for you?

Trying to find his life, Judas lost it.

Unrighteous Mammon

One more comment about Judas: He made money off the crucifixion. I can't think of a more horrifying possibility than to make money off the crucifixion of God's Son.

Money—Jesus called it "unrighteous mammon" (Luke 16:9), meaning there's something inherently sinister in it. Money got Jesus crucified. When you handle it, let your hands tremble and your lips quiver.

> At the cross you're looking at a Man who, because He had everything, could die with nothing.

Looking at both Peter and Judas, we see one big difference between them: Satan had to *ask* permission to sift Peter, but he entered Judas *without even asking* (John 13:27). Why did Satan not need divine permission to enter Judas? I think the answer is connected to the money box.

You see, Judas was Jesus' treasurer. He managed the ministry's money box, which meant he distributed the group's funds as Jesus directed. What's more, he also stole from the box (John 12:6). It's not that stealing was such a horrible sin; the difficulty was that, instead of confessing and repenting, he labored intentionally to hide his sin. Jesus gave him many opportunities to come clean, but he refused to bring his sins into the light. He kept covering up his issues.

Peter, in contrast, was an open book. Peter's issues were just as dark, but he allowed Jesus to see and address them. With him, *what you see is what you get.* Yes, he had a lot of issues, but no secrets.

Secrets. There it is. Judas had secrets. He hid his compulsive stealing from Jesus. He probably thought, *Jesus doesn't even know I'm stealing because, if He knew, He wouldn't give me the money box. Everybody thinks He knows so much, but He doesn't even know His own treasurer is stealing from the box! He's not as omniscient as everyone seems to think He is.*

Judas's refusal to repent and walk in the light meant that, at the most critical juncture of the journey, Satan was able to enter him uninvited and haul him to his destruction.

What do we learn from Judas? Never hide anything from Jesus. Harbor no secrets. Even if you feel trapped by sin and don't know how to overcome, resolve in your heart to walk in the light. Pray something like this: "Jesus, I don't know how to change, but here is my issue. I'm showing it to You. Help me change and overcome!"

Love Him, believe Him, and show Him everything. If you do, He'll bring you through.

For Group Study and Discussion

1. Have you ever experienced what may have been a sifting? Share it with the group.

2. Discuss Peter's faith crisis. Have you ever had a faith crisis? What brought you through?

3. Have you ever experienced a love crisis in your walk with Jesus, in which you questioned His love for you? What helped you overcome?

4. Why do you think Judas betrayed Jesus?

5. Discuss the ominous side of money—"unrighteous mammon" (Luke 16:9). What has the Lord taught you about the evil potential in the love of money?

6. Judas had secrets. In what ways does Scripture encourage us to be transparent before God and others? Search out some verses.

7. As you close your group time, center your prayers around 2 Timothy 3:2.

CHAPTER NINE

Jesus' Seven Sayings

This chapter is devoted to the seven things Jesus said while on the cross. His first saying was recorded by Luke: "Father, forgive them, for they do not know what they do" (Luke 23:34).

Jesus meant that those crucifying Him didn't know what they were doing. Paul wrote about this, saying, "None of the rulers of this age knew; for had they known, they would not have crucified the Lord of glory" (1 Cor 2:8).

But it wasn't just His enemies who didn't know what they were doing; *nobody* that day knew what they were doing. While most biblical expositors consider what His *enemies* didn't know, my meditations are sweet to me when I ponder what His *friends* didn't know. Some of His closest associates and friends did things at the cross that were much more significant than they themselves realized at the time.

Later in this book, we'll look at what Paul called the "enemies of the cross" (Phil 3:18). But here, we're going to look at friends of the cross. Among Jesus' associates, I want to point to three who didn't know the significance of their actions, but yet showed themselves to be friends of the cross.

Three Friends of the Cross

Simon of Cyrene was a friend of the cross who didn't know what he was doing. I call him *a friend of the cross* because he carried the horizontal part of the cross to the crucifixion site for Jesus. Who was he? A traveler from Cyrene (modern-day Libya) who had most likely come to Jerusalem for the Passover. (Passover drew pilgrims from many nations.) He just happened to be passing by at the time Jesus was struggling to carry the post any further. The soldiers pulled Simon out of the crowd and compelled him to carry the beam up to Golgotha.

But Simon didn't know what he was doing. He didn't know he was carrying a cross that we'd be singing about two thousand years later. He didn't know that the post on his shoulder would serve as the lightning rod for God's wrath against sin.

Simon probably thought he was saving Jesus from a burden He couldn't carry. What he didn't know was that, in actuality, Jesus was saving *him* from a burden *he* couldn't carry—all his sins.

As Simon continued to shoulder the beam up the incline, the burden seemed to grow, and sweat broke on his brow. His back bent under the weight, his breathing grew heavier, and his legs pushed harder. As he muscled his way forward, what he didn't know was that the Man in front of him was carrying a much heavier load up that hill—all the sins of the world. On that day, there was sin on no one else in Jerusalem except for the condemned Man stumbling to His execution. He carried our sins, and even more than that, He was actually *made* to be sin for us (2 Cor 5:21).

While carrying that plank, Simon had no idea he was assisting the Champion of heaven as He labored to save our planet. Truly, Simon was among those that day who didn't "know what they do" (Luke 23:34).

Now we come to a *second* friend of the cross who didn't know what she was doing at Christ's passion: Mary of Bethany. I consider her a friend of the cross because she helped prepare Jesus for His burial. Let me remind you what she did.

Mary lived in the town of Bethany with her siblings, Martha and Lazarus. The evening before Jesus would make His triumphal entrance into Jerusalem, the three siblings threw an extravagant feast for Him. His disciples and various guests were also invited. The party was probably a big *Thank-You* to Jesus because, just a few weeks earlier, He had raised Lazarus from the dead.

During the meal, Mary took what may have been her most valuable

Jesus of Nazareth stands before you, Pilate. Be careful, for one day you'll stand before Him.

possession—an expensive and fragrant flask of oil of spike-nard—and emptied its contents on Jesus. He had shown Himself a loyal friend to her and her family, and the smeared oil was her way of showing her gratitude, love, and devotion.

In her mind, Mary was offering love and worship to Jesus, but she didn't know what she was *really* doing. She didn't know that her extravagance was creating a memorial by which she would be honored for all time. Furthermore, she didn't know that, in less than a week, Jesus would be impaled to a cross and killed. Additionally, she didn't know that His death would happen late in the afternoon, precariously close to sundown (when the Sabbath would commence). There wouldn't be enough time to prepare and apply the standard treatment of spices customary to a Jewish burial. Jesus explained what she was really doing: "She has kept this for the day of My burial" (John 12:7).

Mary didn't know that Jesus' burial would be rushed and that she was coming beforehand to anoint His body for burial. Like Simon of Cyrene, she was another at the cross who didn't "know what they do" (Luke 23:34).

And now, we look at a *third* friend of the cross who didn't know what he was doing—Joseph of Arimathea. Who was he? He was a prominent member of the Sanhedrin, a prestigious group of seventy men who served as the supreme court of the Jewish community. When Jesus expired, Joseph solicited Pilate and received permission to bury the body. I consider him a friend of the cross because he took the corpse down from the cross, washed and wrapped it, and laid it in a tomb.

Carefully, he removed the thorns, freed the body from the nails, caught the full weight of the corpse on his shoulder, and gingerly lowered it to the ground. He was probably thinking to himself, *By handling this corpse, I'm now ceremonially defiled, and I won't be able to enter the temple or celebrate this Sabbath.* All he knew was that his neck, arms, and clothes were being dirtied by the blood caked all over Jesus' body. As he handled Jesus' corpse, here's what he didn't know: He was being smeared with the blood of the new covenant! He thought he was being defiled, but instead he was touching the most powerful detergent in the universe. Like Simon and Mary, he was another at the cross who didn't "know what they do" (Luke 23:34). He was being soiled with the blood that was washing away the sins of the world.

Had he known what he was doing, would he have ever washed those clothes?

It wasn't until later that these three friends of the cross—Simon, Mary, and Joseph—understood the nobility of what they had done by honoring Christ at the time of His passion.

You Don't Know What You Do, Either

When you knelt in faith at the foot of the cross, what Jesus said—"They do not know what they do"—was probably also true of you. When you made yourself a friend of the cross and asked for that blood to wash away your sins, you probably didn't know you were touching the uncreated God at the center of His being.

There's nothing God feels more strongly about than the event that occasioned this hemorrhage. Nothing else has ever moved His heart so deeply or impacted His consciousness so profoundly. Why would I say that? Because of the extravagant way He responds to those who place their faith in that cross—and also because of the vehement way He responds to those who dismiss it.

Think about what the Father beheld as He looked at His Son. There was blood on His scalp, blood on His face, blood on His neck, blood on His shoulders, blood on His arms, blood on His hands, blood on His back, blood on His chest, blood on His legs, blood

> If you blame God for all the suffering in the world, that's okay because, on the cross, Jesus took all the blame.

on His feet, blood on His cross, blood on the ground. It was a spectacle of blood. Who can possibly measure what the Father was feeling in that moment?

Here's what you probably didn't know: When you place your faith in Christ and take the cross on your lips, the Father relives everything that happened that day. It all replays before Him as though on a universe-sized, iMax Theater screen. He sees it happening as clearly in front of Him as if it were transpiring in that very moment. When you call on the blood of Jesus, you have no idea the cosmic storm you trigger.

I see this in the Scripture that says, "With the Lord one day is as a thousand years" (2 Pet 3:8). There actually was a day that, to the Lord, seemed to last a *thousand* years. What day was that? The day Christ's flesh splayed on the cross. That day went on, and on, and on. It just *never* seemed to stop. It imprinted the Father's memory so indelibly that He'll never forget any of it.

That same verse goes on to say that with God, "a thousand years is as one day" (2 Pet 3:8). When we look at the cross, we behold an event that, according to our calendar, happened two thousand years ago; but to God, it was *just a couple days ago.* This is why Jesus is portrayed, at the end of this age, as "a Lamb as though it had been slain" (Rev 5:6). Calvary is still so fresh in the Father's memory that, to Him, Jesus was just now slain. This means He hasn't forgotten the slightest modicum of the horror and trauma of that bleak hill. It replays before His eyes as though it happened just yesterday. His emotions about it are as fresh and raw as the moment it happened.

Again, when you first came to the cross, you probably didn't know you were touching God at His most tender place. And this is exactly what makes the cross so powerful! When you call on the name of Jesus and invoke the sprinkling of His blood, the Father turns heaven inside-out for you. It's almost as though He backs a massive dump truck up to your life, lifts the bed, and empties on you the riches of His lovingkindness, the fullness of His mercy, and the abundance of His grace—all because you placed your faith in the blood of Christ's cross.

How could you possibly know your faith would move Him so deeply?

They do not know what they do—what a profound summation of the fact that nobody at Golgotha knew what they were doing. That was Jesus' first saying on the cross. Let's continue our meditations in His seven sayings.

What's Inside Will Come Out

If you want to see what's inside a man, impale him to a tree. Pierce the man and façades disappear. There are no pretenses on a cross. Put nails in the man's hands and feet and whatever's inside will most assuredly come out.

The Roman soldiers were seasoned executioners, and they had watched it happen every time: Puncture the man, and the real person comes out. To say it another way, the language of a crucified victim always revealed the thoughts of their heart—even as Jesus said, "Out of the abundance of the heart the mouth speaks" (Matt 12:34).

When they pierced Jesus, His soul was laid bare and the stuff in His heart came tumbling out of His mouth. The cross revealed what rumbles in the heart of God. What was inside Him? We can find out by contemplating the seven sayings He spoke while crucified. When they punctured Jesus of Nazareth, here's what came out:

1. Forgiveness

As they put nails in His hands and feet, the first thing He had to say was, "Father, forgive them, for they do not know what they do" (Luke 23:34). When they cut Him, He bled *forgiveness*.

Jesus said, Do not worry about tomorrow. Practicing what He preached, He didn't throw Himself into Gethsemane's travail until the day of His crucifixion.

2. Promise

The second thing Jesus said on the cross was a promise uttered to one of the victims crucified with Him. Two thieves were crucified with Jesus, and one of them said to Him, "Lord, remember me when You come into Your kingdom" (Luke 23:42). What would cause him to say this? Well, it's reasonable to suppose he could read the accusation written above Jesus' head: "THE KING OF THE JEWS" (Mark 15:26). The nails didn't make Jesus look much like a King, but strangely enough the thorns seemed to resemble a crown. Faith rose in the thief's heart and he believed he was looking at his King. He believed so strongly that Jesus would come into His kingdom that he confessed it with his mouth (see Rom 10:9). Because of his faith, Jesus extended to him an amazing promise: "Assuredly, I say to you, today you will be with Me in Paradise" (Luke 23:43). Jesus was so full of *promise* that it even came out of Him while enduring incomprehensible suffering.

3. Compassion

Jesus' third saying was a word of compassion for His mother. It seems she was permitted by the soldiers to stand near the foot of the cross, and John came alongside to support her. John recorded the moment when Jesus addressed her:

> When Jesus therefore saw His mother, and the disciple whom He loved standing by, He said to His mother, "Woman, behold your son!" Then He said to the disciple, "Behold your mother!" And from that hour that disciple took her to his own home (John 19:26-27).

Although locked in unfathomable suffering, Jesus drew on His cavernous reserves of compassion and gave instructions concerning His mother's welfare. We could have understood if He had wanted her to care for Him, but instead

He cared for her. When pierced, He couldn't help but bleed *compassion*.

4. Loyalty

In His fourth saying, Jesus quoted David: "My God, My God, why have You forsaken Me?" (Matt 27:46). Having been made sin and a curse for us, Jesus was forsaken of the Father. When He most wanted to feel His Father's nearness, Abba had left Him to the goring bulls. We're struck with amazement, therefore, that even though He was forsaken by the Father in His darkest hour, He still held to His allegiance. When He said, "My God, My God," He was saying, *You are My God.* Although tested by utter forsakenness, His wounds leaked *loyalty*.

5. Longing

John gave us Jesus' fifth saying on the cross:

> After this, Jesus, knowing that all things were now accomplished, that the Scripture might be fulfilled, said, "I thirst!" Now a vessel full of sour wine was sitting there; and they filled a sponge with sour wine, put it on hyssop, and put it to His mouth (John 19:28-29).

David had written, "For my thirst they gave me vinegar to drink," and most interpreters understand that Jesus cried, "I thirst!" so they would bring vinegar to Him in fulfillment of this Scripture (Ps 69:21). However, I think Jesus was speaking not only of His *physical* thirst—stifling as it was—but also of His *spiritual* thirst for His Father. As His body drained of its fluids, He craved His Father's presence. The fifth thing that came out of this pierced victim was *desire* for God.

Jesus spoke of His cross as a baptism because there was no part of His being that didn't suffer.

6. Confidence

Just before He expired, Jesus uttered His sixth saying: "It is finished!" (John 19:30). He meant that the work of the cross was complete and the price for sin was paid in full. He was confident that His Father had finished what He started. This statement showed that, at His impalement, Jesus leaked *confidence* in God.

7. Surrender

When they pierced Jesus, the seventh and final statement that came from His lips was a declaration of surrender. We see this in His last words: "Father, into Your hands I commit My spirit" (Luke 23:46). He surrendered the destiny of His spirit to His Father's providence. We might think that such beautiful submission would carry Jesus' soul to Paradise, but no, He immediately descended to hell. Relinquishment meant that He trusted His Father even if it meant going to hell. His surrender was stunning and complete.

Jesus' last words at His expiration were so compelling that they evoked an exclamation from the centurion who presided over the event. What was a centurion? A seasoned officer who was in charge of one hundred soldiers. Although he had heard just about everything imaginable spilling from crucified victims, never before had he heard such language from a crucified man. Mark 15:39 says, "So when the centurion... saw that He cried out like this...he said, 'Truly this Man was the Son of God!'"

Even the officer charged with crucifying Jesus agreed—His seven sayings were altogether remarkable!

In summary, when they punctured Jesus, here's what came out of Him: forgiveness, promise, compassion, loyalty, longing, confidence, and surrender. These are the things I also want coming out of me when I'm being crucified.

Known in Adversity

Let me say more about that seventh saying, "Into Your hand I commit My spirit." Jesus was quoting Psalm 31:5, which means Psalm 31 was in His thoughts while on the cross. As a *cross psalm*, the entirety of Psalm 31 can be viewed through the lens of the cross. I have a suggestion for you, therefore. Find the time to read Psalm 31, look for the cross in every verse, and talk to God about each verse. Your meditations will likely be sweet to your soul.

Ask the Holy Spirit, *What other verses in this psalm were whispered by Jesus when He was on the cross?* For example, it's probable that Jesus also spoke verse 7 to His Father during His sufferings: "You have known my soul in adversities" (Ps 31:7). Let me share my meditations as I've looked at Psalm 31:7 through the lens of the cross.

When David wrote, "You have known my soul in adversities" (Ps 31:7), he was speaking first of all concerning himself. David suffered many adversities, and his trials caused what was inside him to come out. The thoughts of his heart were expressed in the words he wrote in his psalms (such as Psalm 31), showing who he really was on the inside. When David verbalized in prayer—and then wrote in his psalms— the feelings and thoughts of his heart, the Lord was able to see and know the real David. Adversity opened to a knowing relationship.

But when David penned the words, "You have known my soul in adversities" (Ps 31:7), he wasn't writing only concerning himself; he also seemed to have the cross in view. He was placing these words on the tongue of Christ. During the crucifixion, Jesus said to His Father, "You have known My soul in adversities" (Ps 31:7). In His sufferings, Jesus was known by the Father. When the Father heard Jesus' seven utterances on the cross, He

> We were given power to crush Jesus on the cross, and we still have the ability to break His heart.

must have thought something like, *I knew it! I knew all along that's what was inside You. Your cross only confirms what I knew about You all along.* As is always true, suffering had opened to knowing. The cross opened a dimension of knowing between Father and Son that, if it were possible, was even more profound than ever.

Furthermore, when David wrote, "You have known my soul in adversities" (Ps 31:7), the Holy Spirit had *you* in mind. When *you* suffer adversity, what's inside you will also come out—through the words of your mouth. What you say in your adversity will enable the Father to know *your* soul. Adversity will bring out the real you. As a result of your trials, you'll come into a richer dimension of intimacy with Jesus than you would have otherwise known. And like David, you'll probably find yourself whispering to Jesus, "You have known my soul in adversities."

But the implications of Psalm 31:7 don't stop there. While you're agonizing in your trials, if you'll listen carefully you may hear Jesus saying back to you, "You have known *My* soul in adversities" (Ps 31:7). He means, "As you've walked through your adversities in grace and holiness, you've come to know My soul in a fuller way." Through the course of your sufferings, not only has Jesus come to know your soul, you've also come to know His. Again, adversities will open to knowing. When you endure suffering, you're likely to think, "Oh. Now I see how You feel about the trials You endure, Jesus." Shared sufferings produce intimacy. There are some things about Jesus that can be known only through adversity.

These are some of my thoughts as I've meditated in Psalm 31:7. You can look at the entirety of Psalm 31 is this manner, viewing each verse through the lens of the cross.

The Timing of His Seven Sayings

I examined the *timing* of Jesus' seven sayings and

discovered they were spoken almost like two clusters. He uttered three sayings fairly early in the crucifixion, was silent for a lengthy interim, and then finished up with four sayings at the very end.

The first three sayings were spoken approximately during the first hour of His crucifixion and the last four at the very end, just before His expiration. In-between was a five-hour period in which Jesus quietly went to work.

Someone might wonder why I would place Jesus' words to His mother and John within the first hour of the crucifixion. I join with other students of the cross who take John's words at face value when he wrote, "And from that hour that disciple took her to his own home" (John 19:27). The implication seems to be that Mary was so distraught and over-wrought at her beloved Son's passion that John mercifully took her home *that very hour*. I wonder if he might have said, "Come, Mother. This is too much for you. You can't do this anymore. Come home with me now." Gently pulling her away, he guided to his home an overwhelmingly broken woman who could no longer bear to watch. From that first hour, there's no more mention of Mary being present at the cross or tomb. It was just too much. Truly, a sword had pierced through her soul (Luke 2:35).

I am supposing, therefore, that there was roughly a five-hour period during which Jesus spoke nothing aloud. In those five hours of silence, however, I hear something very loudly: All the things He *didn't* say. He uttered no threats, complaints, bitterness, anger, rage, cursing, self-pity, terror, nor accusation. The silence was deafening. None of those things were in Him, so how could they possibly come out (see John 14:30)?

May none of those things find a home in my heart, either.

Pilate invited the crowd, "Behold the Man!" (John 19:5). That invitation still rumbles through the centuries.

His Sayings Will Advise You

Isaiah called Jesus a *Wonderful Counselor* because He has wonderful counsel for people (Isaiah 9:6). If you'll consult Him while suffering adversity, He'll eagerly coach you through it. How? With His seven sayings on the cross.

In fact, when you're overwhelmed by adversity, you may even feel like you've been *crucified with Christ*. It's almost as though you're on the west face of the cross and He's on the east face. It's almost as though the nails through your hands go through the wood and kiss the nails in His hands.

As you hang suspended in suffering, you should listen carefully because He's speaking from the other side of this cross. The consummate Counselor is coaching you through your trial, telling you what to do.

Jesus has seven pieces of advice as you walk through your trial.

1. Forgive

If you're attentive, you'll hear Him praying, "Father, forgive them, for they do not know what they do" (Luke 23:34). Jesus' first piece of advice for you? *Forgive.* Forgive all who have wronged you. Only when you forgive can you become the person God is shaping through the rejection.

Unforgiveness blocks your view. It clouds your vision and prevents you from perceiving what God is doing in your trial. When you lose sight of God's activity in your adversity, you lose the courage to cooperate with His purposes.

Satan wants you embittered at those who wronged you so that you become a spiritual casualty. On the other hand, Jesus wants you to forgive freely so that you can become a mighty weapon in His hand for delivering others. Forgiveness is the door opener. Entering God's powerful purposes for your fiery trial begins with total forgiveness.

Receive Jesus' advice and put away all bitterness, malice,

resentment, hostility, anger, or hatred. Let forgiveness be the first thing that comes out of you.

2. Hold to promise

You'll be able to hear this one easily because Jesus lifted His voice and said to the dying thief, "Assuredly, I say to you, today you will be with Me in Paradise" (Luke 23:43). What is Jesus' second piece of advice for you during your crucifixion? *Hold to promise.*

When you're crucified with Christ, He'll speak promises to you. He's always promising things to us because He's Promise personified. Promise is a Person (see Luke 24:49) and He just can't help but keep promising you things. Nothing will be more valuable to you in your fiery trial than His "exceedingly great and precious promises" (2 Pet 1:4). His promises are the portal through which you'll experience His divine nature— His compassion, mercy, kindness, goodness, power, gentleness, and generosity.

Prove your promises (Mal 3:10), plead your promises, and protect your promises. Promise will make you crazy bold to hold out for the impossible. A promise from God is like a ticking bomb or like a miracle on a timer. Promise is unstoppable because God's word can't be chained (2 Tim 2:9).

Never let go your promise!

3. Observe the church

You'll hear Jesus' third point of counsel in His words to John and His mother. Once again, here's the passage:

> When Jesus therefore saw His mother, and the disciple whom He loved standing by, He said to His mother, "Woman, behold your son!" Then He said to the disciple, "Behold your mother!" And from that hour that disciple took her to his own home (John 19:26-27).

The Carpenter from Nazareth can chisel the most wooden of hearts.

The woman is the church. In this third cross saying, Jesus actually gives out two points of counsel. First, He says to the church, "Woman, behold your son!" He tells the church to look at you during your suffering. You're a spectacle to both people and angels (1 Cor 4:9), and Jesus allows the church to stand and stare at you. Why? Because her reproach is a necessary ingredient in your journey. She'll look at you with misunderstanding and perplexity, and will form inner judgments about you, all of which is necessary to your spiritual formation.

Second, the words Jesus spoke to John are also intended for your ears: "Behold your mother!" He's telling you to look upon the church and get to know her better. Rather than pulling away because of your pain, you're to draw closer still. Jesus wants you to observe the church from your vantage of suffering. You'll see her as you've never seen her before. You'll gain understanding now that will help you help her later.

4. Inquire into purpose

When Jesus prayed, "My God, My God, why have You forsaken Me?" He was coaching you to inquire into divine purpose (Matt 27:46). He's counseling you to ask God *why*. Ask the hard questions—not because you're questioning His goodness but because you're wanting to understand it. God has strategic purpose in everything He does, and Jesus knows you need to understand His purposes if you're to partner with Him in the adversity.

Jeremiah asked *why* when he said, "Why is my pain perpetual and my wound incurable?" (Jer 15:18). He wanted to understand why there was no respite from his sufferings. God can handle our hard questions, but He wants us to bring them to Him personally. You can ask God almost any question if you ask it to His face. He just doesn't want you complaining about it to others.

Jesus is saying to you, "Come directly to your Father and ask Him the hard why questions. He wants to reveal His purpose to you."

5. Pant after God

Jesus' fifth point of advice for you is in His words, "I thirst!" (John 19:28). As you're crucified with Him, He's telling you to thirst for God. Pursue Him with all your appetites. Hunger and thirst for righteousness, and you'll be filled. Love Him, desire Him, long for Him, and pant for Him as a deer pants for the water brooks (Ps 42:1).

We noted earlier that Jesus probably had Psalm 69:21 in view when He said, "I thirst!" But I wonder if, with arms spread wide, He also had Psalm 143:6 in mind: "I spread out my hands to You; my soul longs for You like a thirsty land. Selah." Spread hands and thirsty longing—it sounds like a cross psalm to me. Notice the Selah in Psalm 143:6. Almost every instance of *Selah* in Psalms can be viewed as pointing to the cross. From now on, whenever you see *Selah* in Psalms, think cross. And pant after Him!

6. Endure to the end

At the end, when Jesus cried, "It is finished!" (John 19:30), hear Him telling you to endure all the way to the very end. Your trial may feel interminable, but there's a time when it's completed, and you'll be able to say with Him, "It is finished." He will complete the good work He has started in you (Phil 1:6).

God had an intended end for Job's trial and He has an intended end for yours, too (James 5:11). Stay in the thing until you enter into your assigned spiritual inheritance. You'll attain that inheritance only through endurance. When Zacharias endured to the end of his trial, he came out prophesying (Luke 1:67); in the same way, when your fiery trial is ended, get ready to prophesy!

> The intensity of the suffering revealed the intensity of the love.

7. Surrender

Listen for Jesus' last piece of advice for you in His words, "Father, into Your hands I commit My spirit" (Luke 23:46). He's telling you to abandon yourself completely to the hands of your beloved Father. He will take the profound death that's been working in you and transform it into resurrection life. You will have lost your life but will have gained it for eternal life.

Jesus spoke four of His seven sayings directly to His Father, which shows us where His gaze was fixed throughout the ordeal. Thus, the Wonderful Counselor is showing you, in your sufferings, where to look. Keep your gaze entirely upon your Father!

To recap, here's Jesus counsel to you while you're crucified with Him: *Forgive. Hold to promise. Observe the church. Inquire into purpose. Pant after God. Endure to the end. Surrender.*

Thank You, Wonderful Counselor, for showing us seven ways to run our race well.

For Group Study and Discussion

1. What do you think it means to be a friend of the cross?

2. Do you think the Father is more passionate about the cross than anything else? Talk about Bob's premise that, when we call on the blood of Calvary, the Father relives that event. Is this what makes the blood of Christ so powerful?

3. In what ways do you see 2 Peter 3:8 pointing to the cross?

4. *When suffering, what's inside comes out.* How has this been true in your own journey with God?

5. Take some time this week to study the seven sayings of Jesus on the cross, and bring your observations to the group discussion.

6. What insight might you have regarding the roughly five hours of Christ's silence on the cross?

7. As you close the group, choose one of Jesus' seven sayings as the center of your prayer time.

CHAPTER TEN

Our Substitute

What Jesus did for us on the cross is often called a *substitutionary* work because He took our place on the cross. We should have died there for our sin, but instead, He did.

The cross is God doing for us what we couldn't do for ourselves. We couldn't save ourselves so He came to our rescue. In fact, He did it singlehandedly. That point is emphasized in Hebrews 1:3, speaking of "when He had *by Himself* purged our sins." He had this one, all by Himself. We couldn't help Him purge our sins, and we still can't help Him save us. It's all of Him from start to finish.

All we could do was crucify Him, He did the rest.

Paul wrote that "Christ died for us" (Rom 5:8). Notice the word *for*—it's the linchpin word in many Scriptures regarding Christ serving as our substitute. He suffered *for* us, in our place, so we wouldn't have to.

When Jesus died for us, Calvary became a mountain of contradictions. Life died; good was defeated; righteousness became sin; light was overcome by darkness; God was God-forsaken; the Blessed One was cursed. But through His power, God redeemed every contradiction. Life died—and we who were dead now live. Righteousness became sin—and we who were bound in iniquity now become the righteousness of God by faith. He was cursed so that we, who were under the curse of sin, can be eternally blessed. The glory of what He's done for us can't possibly be overstated. The substitutionary work of Christ deserves our highest praise and greatest gratitude!

We were trying to kill Him for centuries, and when we finally managed it, we were stunned to discover His death meant our life. How can we possibly comprehend this kind of love?

We are speaking of what theologians

I drew His blood, then He washed me with it.

sometimes call the *substitutionary atonement of the cross*. No Scripture makes it clearer than 1 Peter 3:18, "For Christ also suffered once for sins, the just for the unjust, that He might bring us to God." He suffered for our sins so that we never have to.

When we explore the ways Christ suffered for us, we're peering into some of the most sublime truths of our gospel. These are the themes that inspire sermons, songs, books, poems, prayers, and more. Let's stay with this theme for a little while, therefore, and consider some of the glorious ways in which Christ suffered *for* us so we don't have to.

Aspects of His Substitutionary Work

- He bore the curse of the law for us.

The law *(Torah)* of Moses bestowed many wonderful blessings on those who obeyed it and many curses on those who disobeyed it. For those who wanted to receive the law's blessings, there was a killer caveat: You had to obey every single *Torah* law perfectly, down to the last letter. If you disobeyed even one of those laws, you forfeited the blessings and became subject to the curses assigned to the disobedient. It was performance-based religion, and nobody could perform adequately. The law had become a curse to us, and we needed someone to deliver us from this curse.

Only Jesus could pull this one off. First, He came to earth as a Man and fulfilled the law perfectly. Then, when He died, He didn't have to die for His own sin because He was sinless. As an innocent Lamb, He was not under the curse of the law, so He could absorb the curse that was on us and bear our punishment in our place. On the cross, He actually became a curse for us so we could be blessed:

> Christ has redeemed us from the curse of the law, having
> become a curse for us (for it is written, *"Cursed is everyone who*

hangs on a tree"), that the blessing of Abraham might come upon the Gentiles in Christ Jesus, that we might receive the promise of the Spirit through faith (Gal 3:13-14).

Jesus became a curse for us, and now we are eternally blessed by God. *Jesus, thank You for reversing our curse!*

- He carried our griefs and sorrows for us.

Isaiah testified, "Surely He has borne our griefs and carried our sorrows" (Isa 53:4). Instead of being incarcerated in grief and sorrow, we now share in His comfort and joy.

- He was scourged for our healing.

When we believe in His work on the cross, we are healed from all sickness and disease. Peter quoted Isaiah 53:5 when he wrote, "Who Himself bore our sins in His own body on the tree, that we, having died to sins, might live for righteousness—by whose stripes you were healed" (1 Pet 2:24). Jesus took every kind of sickness and disease in His body so that we can be healed and made whole. This is a fantastic gospel!

- He took the punishment for our sins.

When we place our faith in the cross, we're forgiven and experience no punishment for sin. This truth was so large for Isaiah that in Isaiah 53 he spoke of it six times (vv. 5, 6, 8, 10, 11, 12). For example, verse 8 says, "For the transgressions of My people He was stricken." Jesus' crucifixion was utterly horrific, demonstrating that the punishment for our sins was monstrous. And yet, He absorbed that horrible punishment so we wouldn't have to. He's so kind!

Some people get angry at God because they blame Him for all the pain and suffering in the world. But that's okay because, at the cross, Jesus took all the

He never meant for us to look on the cross and weep (Luke 23:28), but to look on the cross and believe.

blame. Now, nobody need ever suffer the blame for the pain and suffering they've caused.

- He bore the wrath of God for us.

John said that God sent Jesus to be "the propitiation for our sins" (1 John 4:10). *Propitiation* means appeasement. Jesus appeased God's wrath against sin by absorbing it until it was wrung out. In the beautiful words of Erwin Lutzer, "God's justice had spent all of its ammunition; there is nothing left to be hurled at us."[1] The cross was a lightning rod for God's wrath and now we don't ever have to bear that wrath.

- He was condemned in our place.

What does it mean to be condemned? According to Scripture, it means to be sentenced forever to death and hell. Jesus was condemned and went to hell so we never have to. This is why Romans 8:1 says, "There is therefore now no condemnation to those who are in Christ Jesus." He was condemned to death, descended to hell, overcame Hades and death, and resurrected in power so that we need never be condemned ourselves. *Jesus, we love You!*

- He absorbed loneliness for us.

He died in complete loneliness so that, when we place our faith in Him, we can live with Him forever. When we're joined to Him, He assures us, "I will never leave you nor forsake you" (Heb 13:5). With His companionship, we're never alone. Ever.

- Jesus was made sin for us.

Consequently, when we believe in Christ, we are freed from sin and made the righteousness of God. Paul described it this way:

---

1 Erwin W. Lutzer, *Cries From The Cross*. (Chicago: Moody Press, 2002), 122.

"For He made Him who knew no sin to be sin for us, that we might become the righteousness of God in Him" (2 Cor 5:21). He lost everything so we could receive everything. When you see the heights of the righteousness to which your filthy heart has been lifted, the majesty of the cross becomes overwhelming. Our faith in the cross gives God the capital He needs to present us faultless before His throne with great glory and joy (Jude 1:24).

Calvary doesn't simply give God the *option* of forgiving the people He feels warmly inclined toward; it *requires* Him to forgive every single penitent sinner who calls on His name. Justice demands that we be forgiven. In other words, when you repent of your sin, it's *impossible* to be denied His forgiveness. Therefore, let every human being call on His name!

Jesus Endured Racism for Us

When I consider the many ways Christ suffered for us on the cross, I'm reminded that He also suffered racial hatred in our place.

At the time of this writing, racial tensions are high in America. In response, I'd like to show how Christ suffered racism at the cross. He suffered it *for* us so we could be freed from its sinister grip. Let me explain where I see racism in Christ's sufferings.

Racial issues swirled around the cross. For example, Asians arrested Jesus, Europeans crucified Him, and an African carried His cross up the hill. Asians are mostly brown, Europeans are mostly white, and Africans are mostly black. All shades of skin and all three continents were represented on Golgotha. Additionally, the accusation above Christ's head was written in three languages (Greek, Latin, and Hebrew). It truly was an international event.

> The cross opens the most preposterous possibility imaginable: God now justifies the ungodly (Rom 4:5).

I wonder if the Roman soldiers

compelled Simon to carry Jesus' cross because he was black. As an ethnic minority, he would have stood out in the crowd. Racism was as alive back then as it is today.

Roman people hated Jews. Pilate despised his Jerusalem assignment because the Jews were so confoundedly non-compliant. When Roman soldiers got stationed in Jerusalem, they mourned their foul fortune. The setting was ripe for the cross to become a brouhaha of racial animosity.

When the Roman soldiers received a free pass to do whatever they wanted to Jesus, they vented their racial venom on Him. They went way beyond the book. They even put thorns on His head and pounded them into His skull with a reed. The purple robe, the scourging, the thorns—all were intensified by racial prejudice.

Jesus simply absorbed it all with a demeanor that seemed to say, *There's nothing you can do to Me to make Me hate you. There's nothing you can do to Me to make Me angry, threatening, or vindictive. It doesn't matter what you do to Me, I love you.*

Jesus took the blows of racism for us and paid its price. In Christ, we're freed from the tentacles of hatred and liberated into the limitless love of Christ.

The cross is the answer to racism (and virtually every social evil). Why? Because of the selfless love it demonstrates. The love of the cross puts to death any confidence in the flesh and lays down its life for anyone, regardless of racial ancestry.

The cross is the great equalizer. Regardless of our ethnicity, at the cross we're all sinners equally in need of a Savior. When we repent, we're all washed in the same fountain and adopted into the same family. Just as creation made us all one blood in the flesh, the cross makes us all one blood in the Spirit.

As already detailed in chapter six, when the love of Christ fills us, we could wish ourselves accursed from Christ forever if it could mean the eternal salvation of our fellow countrymen (see Rom 9:3). This love has no regard to political affiliation, skin color, gender, or economic privilege. The love of the cross empowers us to love one another, prefer one another, esteem others better than ourselves, and lay our lives down for one another (Phil 2:3).

When you encounter people of other ethnicities, languages, and skin colors, do you find yourself wishing to be accursed from Christ if it could mean their salvation? If so, the love of the cross has found its way into your heart.

May this love find entrance in *every* heart today. Jesus bore the venom of racism so that His love could fill every heart in every nation. It bears repeating: The love of the cross is the answer for racial hatred.

What a Glorious Message!

When we behold the substitutionary atonement of Christ, all we can do is worship. This theme makes for the best songs and the highest praise. Christ's substitutionary atonement has inspired the greatest songs of redemptive hymnology. What hymn shall I use to illustrate this? Allow me to quote my father's favorite hymn:

> I will sing of my Redeemer
> And His wondrous love to me;
> On the cruel cross He suffered,
> From the curse to set me free.
>
> Sing, O sing of my Redeemer,
> With His blood He purchased me,
> On the cross He sealed my pardon,
> Paid the debt, and made me free.[2]

One of the most beautiful statements about Christ's atonement was written by John R. W. Stott in his classic work, *The Cross of Christ*:

We're delivered by the Lion so we can marry the Lamb.

2   *I Will Sing of My Redeemer,* by Philip P. Bliss, 1876.

I could never myself believe in God, if it were not for the cross. In the real world of pain, how could one worship a God who was immune to it? A Buddha sits legs crossed, arms folded, eyes closed, the ghost of a smile playing round his mouth, a remote look on his face, detached from the agonies of the world. But in my mind I have to turn instead to that lonely, twisted, tortured figure on the cross, nails through hands and feet, back lacerated, limbs wrenched, brow bleeding from thorn-pricks, mouth dry and intolerably thirsty, plunged in God-forsaken darkness. That is the God for me! He laid aside His immunity to pain. He entered our world of flesh and blood, tears and death. He suffered for us. The cross of Christ is God's only self-justification in such a world as ours.[3]

Yes, when we meditate upon the substitutionary death of Christ, we are gazing upon some of the most glorious truths of our gospel. What a majestic cross, where He suffered so we never have to!

This is the part of the cross we sing about the most, preach about the most, and celebrate the most because it's gloriously wonderful!

However, it's only half our message. There's another side to the cross to also understand and explore. To see my meaning, come to the next chapter.

---

3   John R.W. Stott, *The Cross of Christ.* (Downers Grove, IL: InterVarsity Press, 1986), 335-336.

For Group Study and Discussion

1. Read Luke 22-24 this week, and share with the group what moved you most in this reading of the crucifixion account.

2. As our substitute, Christ died *for* us. Find at least three Scriptures that testify to this truth, and then share them with the group at the meeting.

3. Can you share with the group the lyrics of a song or poem that points to Christ's substitutionary death for us?

4. This chapter mentions several aspects of His substitutionary work. Which one resonates most strongly with you right now, and why?

5. Talk about ways in which the cross addresses racism. How can we present the cross as the answer to racial hatred?

6. Read aloud the quote from John R.W. Stott, and say what it means to you.

7. As we close the group, let's pray for anyone needing divine healing in their body. Pray from 1 Peter 2:24.

CHAPTER ELEVEN

Two Sides to the Cross

There are two sides to the cross. First of all, as discussed in the previous chapter, there's the *substitutionary nature* of the cross. This side contains the most grisly aspects of Christ's sufferings in which He experienced a living hell so we would never have to. This is the side we usually speak about when sharing the gospel with seekers, or when establishing believers in the fundamental truths of the gospel, or when nurturing faith for healing, deliverance, provision, and answered prayer.

This side of the cross is absolutely magnificent, and I'm incapable of speaking adequately of its glory, riches, and meaning. *Blessed be the Lamb of God for dying in our place!*

But the *substitutionary nature* of the cross is not our only message. There's another side to the cross—what I call the *identificational nature* of the cross. This is the side of the cross where we identify with and share in His sufferings. As Paul wrote, "I have been crucified with Christ" (Gal 2:20). This is the side of the cross He navigated in order to show us how. He's our Olympic Champion and Trainer who ran the race before us and now coaches us to run the same course successfully.

The substitutionary side is by far the heavier side of the cross. On that side, Jesus did all the heavy lifting. In contrast, the identificational side of the cross that we're invited to share is both easy and light (Matt 11:30). Since our afflictions are both light and momentary, we consider it incredibly dignifying to share with Christ in this side of the cross (2 Cor 4:17).

Both the substitutionary and identificational sides are brought together in one verse masterfully by Peter: "For to this you were called, because Christ also suffered for us, leaving us an example, that you should follow His steps" (1 Pet 2:21). Peter first acknowledged that Christ suffered "for" us, which points to His vicarious, substitutionary suffering. But then Peter went on to describe the identificational nature of the cross when he added, "leaving us an example, that you should follow His steps." In His sufferings, Jesus charted a path for us to follow.

In one brief verse, Peter helped us see that the cross is both substitutionary and identificational.

Two chapters later, Peter brought these two together again: "Therefore, since Christ suffered for us in the flesh, arm yourselves also with the same mind" (1 Pet 4:1). He reiterated that Christ suffered "for" us (substitutionary) with the consequence that we should have "the same mind" (identificational).

One reason we haven't always understood the characteristics that distinguish the substitutionary and identificational sides of the cross is because, at first glance, they appear contradictory. They're profoundly paradoxical. A paradox is two truths that appear, on the surface, to contradict—but ultimately their juxtaposition opens to a more robust understanding of truth.

The contradiction has us asking, "Does the cross *save* us from suffering, or does it *lead* us into suffering?" The answer, paradoxically, is *both*. The substitutionary side saves us from suffering the consequences of sin, and the identificational side offers us the privilege of suffering with Jesus in the war zone of this world.

Our gospel is full of paradoxes. In his letters to the Corinthians, Paul wrote about how he had personally experienced many of those paradoxes. For example, he had a lot to say about the paradox between death and life—between crucifixion and resurrection.

Should Christians expect to experience the death of the cross in their daily lives, or the energizing life of the resurrection? Paradoxically, Paul said we can expect to experience *both* on a regular basis.

Feel buried by adversity? No one knows better than Jesus what it feels like to need resurrecting.

On the one hand, he said, "I die daily"; but then he went on to add, "For we also are weak in Him, but we shall live with Him by the power of God toward you" (1 Cor 15:31; 2 Cor. 13:4).

Both death and resurrection life seemed to be Paul's normative, daily experience. For example, he wrote, "Always carrying about in the body the dying of the Lord Jesus, that the life of Jesus also may be manifested in our body" (2 Cor 4:10). He was always dying and always living. You can't get much more paradoxical than that!

As paradoxical as it seems, the life of faith is a daily participation in both the substitutionary and identificational aspects of the cross—at the same time.

Enemies of the Cross

Disciples of Jesus would never consider themselves enemies of the cross, and yet Paul said its enemies are *many*:

> For many walk, of whom I have told you often, and now tell you even weeping, that they are the enemies of the cross of Christ: whose end is destruction, whose god is their belly, and whose glory is in their shame—who set their mind on earthly things (Phil 3:18-19).

Paul said he spoke *often* to them of these enemies, indicating this was an important emphasis in his apostolic teachings. He said there are many enemies of the cross who walk a path that doesn't follow Jesus' steps.

Now, no believer is an enemy of the *substitutionary* nature of the cross—the sufferings He endured so we would never have to. When we consider that He took sin's punishment in our place, or that He took our sicknesses in His stripes so we can be healed, or that He absorbed God's wrath so we can be free of condemnation, *everybody* is a friend of that side of the cross.

Of what, then, are they enemies? They're enemies of the

identificational nature of the cross—the side of the cross that compels us to suffer with Him. Now don't get me wrong, I dislike suffering just as much as you. Not even Jesus wanted to suffer. *Nobody* in a human body likes to suffer. But when we recoil from sharing in Christ's sufferings, we make ourselves enemies of the cross.

Enemies of the cross position themselves in a stance that ends in destruction. The issues here are eternal and, therefore, of utmost importance. There seems to be a connection between Philippians 3:18-19 and what Paul wrote a few verses earlier:

> That I may know Him and the power of His resurrection, and the fellowship of His sufferings, being conformed to His death, if, by any means, I may attain to the resurrection from the dead (Phil 3:10-11).

Enemies of the cross are believing unbelievers who see the cross as Jesus' best way forward but not their own. They receive its benefits but not its constraints. They're eager to know Christ in the power of His resurrection but unwilling to know Him in the fellowship of His sufferings, "whose end is destruction" (Phil 3:19).

Barabbas Was an Enemy of the Cross

Sometimes I wonder if we bear a stronger resemblance to Barabbas than Jesus. You'll recall that Barabbas was freed from his death sentence by the cross. With his condemnation lifted, he skipped jubilantly into the freedom the cross gave him. But now, do I look more like Barabbas—nailed to nothing? While Christ is being impaled to the will of God, have I absconded on a liberation romp?

Paul never expressed a desire to look like Barabbas, running free in boundless joy. Rather, he wrote, "[I want to be]

> When your hands are nailed to a tree, you don't hold onto anything of this world.

conformed to His death, if, by any means, I may attain to the resurrection from the dead" (Phil 3:10-11). Paul was saying, *I want to look like Christ in His death.* Picture the mangled, contorted body of Christ on the cross as He drew His final breath; Paul said he wanted his life to look like *that.* Why? So that he could, "if by any means, attain to the resurrection from the dead." Paul knew that if he shared in His death he would also share in His resurrection (see Rom 6:5).

Every once in a while, I want to hold a mirror to my life and ask, who do I more closely resemble? Liberated Barabbas or impaled Jesus?

Your flesh is Barabbas, set free by the cross. And since your flesh is an enemy of the cross, it now loves to quote 1 Corinthians 6:12, "All things are lawful for me." Your flesh is thrilled that the cross has made you free to do whatever you want.

Friends of the cross, however, are inclined differently. They have "crucified the flesh with its passions and desires" (Gal 5:24). Yes, friends of the cross celebrate the freedom from sin the cross has given them, but they also submit to the constraints of the nails.

Paul wrote about the enemies of the cross with tears. Why was he weeping? Because he understood the tragedy of what they were forfeiting.

- Enemies of the cross forfeit the solidarity of suffering with Jesus.

Sharing the cross brings us into profound intimacy with Christ. We'll never know Him in fullness until we go with Him to the cross. Being scarred by the same thing produces brotherhood, closeness, friendship, mutual understanding, and more. Enemies of the cross forfeit this bond.

- Enemies of the cross forfeit an eternal perspective on life.

Paul described the enemies of the cross as those "whose

god is their belly...who set their mind on earthly things"
(Phil 3:19). They're people of the world who live for the
ephemeral rather than the eternal. The advantage of temporary rewards is that they're experienced here and now, and are
the envy of our friends. In contrast, the advantage of eternal
rewards is that they're ours forever—even if they're not seen
or experienced in this life. And in actuality, the light afflictions of the cross are "but for a moment," and they work for
us "a far more exceeding and eternal weight of glory" (2 Cor
4:17). Enemies of the cross forfeit this eternal perspective on
fiery trials.

- Enemies of the cross forfeit their spiritual inheritance

Because Jesus did the cross, the Father said, "Therefore
I will divide Him a portion with the great, and He shall divide the spoil with the strong, because He poured out His soul
unto death" (Isa 53:12). The cross was the portal to Christ's
greater inheritance, and the same is true for us. Enemies of
the cross forfeit the marvelous spiritual portion the Father
designs for them.

- Enemies of the cross forfeit resurrection.

When Paul said their "end is destruction" (Phil 3:19), he
meant that the enemies of the cross forfeit resurrection. No
cross no resurrection. The enemies of the cross suffer such
devastating losses that it's little wonder Paul wept as he wrote
about it.

Jesus, make me a friend of Your cross!

The Repellent Truths of the Gospel

When you contemplate the prospect
of sharing in the sufferings of the cross,
you're certainly not alone if you find your
flesh shrinking back. This is the part of

> The cross brought togeth-
> er unbending absolutes
> and over-bending kind-
> ness (Ps 85:10).

our gospel message that goes down hard. Again, *nobody* likes to suffer.

Not all gospel truths are equally palatable. Most are delightful and exhilarating, but some are bitter and challenging to embrace. The delightful truths mostly align with the substitutionary nature of the cross and the bitter with the identificational side. For gospel messengers to be faithful to their calling, they must preach both the popular and unpopular aspects of the gospel.

We have an illustration of the unpalatable side of the gospel in the Passover lamb. At Passover, the Israelites were told to eat the entire lamb that had been roasted in fire. They were to eat the whole lamb, entrails included (Exod 12:8-10). Some of the lamb's body parts were delicious, but other parts were pungent. They were required to eat both the savory and unsavory. This foreshadowed the gospel, in which we obey both the delightful and difficult commands of Christ.

In his farewell talk with the Ephesian elders, Paul testified, "For I have not shunned to declare to you the whole counsel of God" (Acts 20:27). The word *shunned* would hint at something unsavory. Paul meant that, in declaring the whole counsel of God, he taught both the bitter and sweet elements of the gospel. He didn't withhold truths that were challenging to hear. In other words, he was a faithful messenger of the whole gospel, both the pleasant and the unpleasant.

Paul added, however, that some coming after him would speak "perverse things" because of their desire "to draw away the disciples after themselves" (Acts 20:30). Those who want to grow a following usually bypass the repellent elements of the gospel because speaking those truths thins out one's following.

Jesus died a naked, penniless martyr; His disciples aspire to the same. But such an aspiration is repellent to the flesh.

What might be another example of the repellent nature of discipleship? Fasting. Jesus fasted from food, and so do His disciples (see Mark 2:20). In contrast, enemies of the cross aren't likely to fast because their god is their belly (Phil 3:19). The world denies its belly nothing, but disciples deny themselves in order to partner more fully with Jesus' purposes in the earth. Fasting is unsavory in the swallowing but can produce sweet rewards of fruitfulness in the end.

To speak of suffering strikes some as morbid or repugnant, but the end is always resurrection—powerful, energizing, life-giving resurrection. True life!

In balancing the two sides of the cross, most authors, songwriters, and preachers tend to emphasize the substitutionary nature of the cross. Therefore, I want to help us find our balance by highlighting that which tends to get overlooked by some. Whatever you do, don't close this book now. Come with me as we use the next four chapters to take a closer look at the identificational nature of the cross.

> Jesus died a naked, penniless martyr; are you sure you want to follow Him?

For Group Study and Discussion

1. How would you define, in your own words, the difference between the substitutionary and identificational sides of the cross? How has seeing this distinction helped you?

2. Discuss the paradox found in the truth that Christ suffered so we don't have to, but also suffered so that now we get to. How is this paradox helping you see the cross more fully?

3. In what way have you experienced both the dying and resurrection of Christ in the same season?

4. How can we avoid being an enemy of the cross?

5. What statement in this chapter struck you with the most impact?

6. What would you consider to be some of the repellent truths of the gospel?

7. As you close, use 1 Peter 2:21 in your prayers for each other.

CHAPTER TWELVE
Shared Sufferings

J esus has invited us to take up our cross and follow Him. We're eager to accept the invitation because lovers want to do *everything* together—even the hard stuff. He has suffered for us in ways we'll never have to and now, in gratitude and affection, we want to share the journey with Him. All of life becomes a romantic adventure as we build a shared history together.

As already said, mutual suffering produces an uncommon bond of loyalty and solidarity. This idea is a familiar theme in many movies. For example, in movies such as *The Way Back (2010), Robin Hood Prince of Thieves,* or *Shawshank Redemption,* the plot centers around a small band of prisoners who develop an unusual fidelity to one another because of their common sufferings. In a similar way, when we suffer with Christ, we're joined to Him in profound ways.

I see an example of this pattern in my marriage. Eleven years after our wedding, I suffered a debilitating vocal injury that rocked our world. Marci chose to step into the prison with me, and consequently, we've walked territory together that no one else knows about. Now, nobody else could ever take her place in my life. Our history of shared suffering has given us an irreplaceable bond.

The same thing happens between Christ and His bride. When we experience His sufferings and partner with His purposes, we develop a camaraderie that no other creation shares—not even angels, cherubim, or seraphim. In fact, these creatures look at the romantic adventure we enjoy with Jesus and gaze upon it with curious wonder.

For two thousand years, the church has suffered with Christ. In the early years of the church, when the fires of persecution were real hot, church elders were asked if they were willing to die for Christ. Their vows of consecration included these words:

"Are thou then able to drink of the cup which I am about to drink or be baptized with the baptism with which I am about to be baptized?"

To which they answered, "I take on myself scourgings, imprisonment, tortures, reproaches, crosses, blows, tribulation, and all the temptations of the world which our Lord, and Intercessor, and the Catholic and Apostolic Holy Church took upon themselves." Suffering for Christ was considered normative.

In that same spirit, John Wesley would tell the pastors in his burgeoning movement, "Always be ready to pray, always be ready to preach, and always be ready to die."

When you suffer with Christ, you join the ranks of a great cloud of witnesses who have drunk a cup with Christ and now have a compelling story of God's faithfulness and grace in their lives.

See the Verse through the Cross

My meditations in Scripture have often been sweetened by this exercise: I'll take the verse I'm reading, imagine it emblazoned over the cross, and then meditate on it in that light. I'll consider how the verse might give fresh perspective to the cross. I've done that, for example, with Hebrews 1:5, "I will be to Him a Father, and He shall be to Me a Son."

Placed over the cross, that verse tells me God was fathering Jesus on Golgotha and Jesus was being a true Son. How does God father His sons? I find my answer at the cross. He takes them through a great death so He can lift them to a great resurrection. That was His way with Jesus, and it's still His way with His children.

When He's fathering you in this manner, everyone will stare at you and speculate. Then, at just the right time, He'll raise you up, crown you with glory and

> How can you experience a compelling resurrection unless you've first known an agonizing crucifixion?

honor, and vindicate you before the cynics. If this was His way with Jesus, then why not with you, too?

He will be a faithful Father to you. If suffering should come your way, prove yourself a true son or daughter.

The Accuser Hates Your Father

The accuser will tell you that Abba's fatherhood is oppressive, heavy-handed, and tyrannical. He all but said this to Jesus in the forty-day wilderness temptation. He implied, "Your Father says that, if You do the cross, He'll give You the whole world. But I'll make You an even better offer. If You'll worship me, I'll give it all to You here and now. All I ask is that You worship me. That's not enough for Your Father, but it's enough for me. If you let me, I'll be a better father to you than Your Abba. Just worship me and boom, it's all Yours instantly."

Jesus' response was basically, "I'm going with My heavenly Father. I'm going His way, the way of the cross, because I know His leadership is perfect."

Satan's wisdom said, *Lose Your life and...You'll lose Your life.*

The Father's wisdom said, *Lose Your life and You'll find it.*

Cynics look at God's fathering style at the cross and call it cosmic child abuse. To that criticism I would say: If the cross had been the last chapter in Jesus' story, then yes, it would have been cosmic child abuse. But the cross was only a chapter in the story. The Father demonstrated His kindness by raising Christ from the dead and giving Him a name above every other name. Yes, the Father crucifies His sons, but He also resurrects them.

The cross is never meant to be your last chapter!

We don't learn about the cross academically in a library, but experientially in the lab of life. God doesn't simply reveal it to us; He works it in us. We learn the cross *identificationally.*

To a Certain Extent

The cross is experienced in percentages. To understand my meaning, look at 1 Peter 4:13, "Rejoice to the extent that you partake of Christ's sufferings, that when His glory is revealed, you may also be glad with exceeding joy." Look especially at the words, "to the extent." When we suffer with Christ, we are partaking of His sufferings *to only a certain extent.*

No one has ever identified 100 percent with Christ's cross. We're totally incapable of bearing such a burden. We're able to bear His sufferings only to a limited extent—to a certain percentage.

When we're in a fiery trial, we're partaking of Christ's sufferings to only a limited degree. For example, I can suppose the Lord thinking that our identification with the sufferings of Christ might account for 10 percent or 20 percent of our ordeal (or whatever the percentage). The other 80 percent or 90 percent of our trial might be accounted for by our mistakes, our sins, other people's sins, accidental happenings, etc. But to whatever extent you're partaking of Christ's sufferings, Peter told us to rejoice—"that when His glory is revealed, you may also be glad with exceeding joy."

How can we know if, in our troubles, we're partaking in Christ's sufferings to some extent? I find the answer a few verses later in Peter: "Therefore let those who suffer according to the will of God commit their souls to Him in doing good, as to a faithful Creator" (1 Pet. 4:19). When we "suffer according to the will of God," then we are partaking in Christ's sufferings.

Are you suffering according to the will of God? To ask it another way, is it God's will that you experience this trial? Then rejoice, for you are identifying with Him in His cross to some extent. This is the identificational nature of the cross.

Paul had a thorn in his flesh (2 Cor 12:7), but Jesus had many thorns in His flesh. Our sufferings are but a fraction of His.

Endure and Embrace

When you're sharing in Christ's sufferings, you may be told by someone to "embrace the cross," because that kind of sentiment is common in the body of Christ today. They may say things like, *Embrace the crushing. Embrace the discipline. Embrace the fiery trial.*

When they said that to me, I didn't know what to do with it because I have promises of being healed from the affliction. How could I embrace something when I'm in a fight of faith to be healed of it?

This tension tore my soul for years, until the Lord gave me an answer from two verses in the book of Hebrews. The first verse was this:

> Looking unto Jesus, the author and finisher of our faith, who for the joy that was set before Him endured the cross, despising the shame, and has sat down at the right hand of the throne of God (Heb 12:2).

It doesn't say that Jesus *embraced* the cross, but that He *endured* the cross. How can you embrace a cross when your hands are nailed to it? You could say He embraced the horizontal beam when He carried it toward Calvary, but regarding the crucifixion itself, He didn't embrace the wood, He was nailed to it. Now here's the second verse:

> These all died in faith, not having received the promises, but having seen them afar off were assured of them, embraced them and confessed that they were strangers and pilgrims on the earth (Heb 11:13).

This verse says the heroes of faith embraced *promises.* Promises are something to wrap your arms around and never let go. When God gives you a precious promise, never let it get away from your grip. Promises are to be embraced; the cross is to be endured.

By putting those two verses together, here's the wisdom the Lord gave me: Endure the discipline, embrace the promise.

Psalm 91

I see the identificational nature of the cross depicted beautifully in Psalm 91. Let me show it to you.

God's promises to Abraham were made first and foremost not to Abraham but to Jesus. That's what Paul said in Galatians 3:16, "Now to Abraham and his Seed were the promises made. He does not say, 'And to seeds,' as of many, but as of one, 'And to your Seed,' who is Christ." When God made promises to Abraham, He actually had Jesus in mind (who is Abraham's descendant). In fact, *all* the promises of the Old Testament were intended for Jesus first.

Therefore, when looking at the promises of Psalm 91, keep in mind they were given first of all to Christ. That means Psalm 91:11-12 were intended primarily for Him:

> For He shall give His angels charge over you, to keep you in all your ways. In their hands they shall bear you up, lest you dash your foot against a stone.

When Satan quoted that verse to Jesus in the wilderness temptation, he was correct in insinuating that promise belonged to Him (Matt 4:6). Conveniently though, Satan stopped short of quoting the next verse! "You shall tread upon the lion and the cobra, the young lion and the serpent you shall trample underfoot" (Ps 91:13). Why didn't Satan remind Jesus of *that* part of the promise, too? He seems to have mastered this business of picking and choosing the verses that suit his fancy.

Now, here's the part of Psalm 91 I want to highlight:

> We have a cross, a book, and a King. It's enough.

> Because he has set his love upon Me, therefore I will deliver him; I will set him on high, because he has known My name. He shall call upon Me, and I will answer him; I will be with him in trouble; I will deliver him and honor him. With long life I will satisfy him, and show him My salvation (Ps 91:14-16).

In this passage, the Father was prophesying over Jesus as He hung on the cross. The carnal mind doesn't see the passage in that light because there are aspects of these promises that don't seem to fit the cross. Here are some ways the passage doesn't appear, on the surface, to apply to the cross:

1. "Therefore I will deliver him": Jesus wasn't delivered from the death of the cross.

2. "I will answer him": We have no record of the Father answering Jesus while on the cross.

3. "I will be with him in trouble": Rather than staying with Him, the Father forsook Him.

4. "With long life I will satisfy him": But Jesus lived only to age thirty-three.

But when we realize the cross and resurrection are all one great event wrapped together, then we can see Psalm 91:14-16 being relevant to the cross. Here are the answers I see:

1. "Therefore I will deliver him": It's true that Jesus wasn't delivered from the death of the cross, but that's because the Father wanted to deliver Him from something far greater. To be delivered simply from the cross was too small a thing in the Father's eyes. The Father was looking for something far more dramatic for His beloved Son. He chose to deliver Him instead from death, hell, and the grave.

2. "I will answer him": True, the Father didn't answer Jesus

while on the cross, because Jesus had not yet sunk low enough. The Father waited until Jesus had descended to hell, and then He answered Him there (Ps 22:21). He answered Him by raising Him up from hell.

3. "I will be with him in trouble": It's true that the Father forsook Jesus on the cross. And yet, in the mystery and vastness of God's greatness, He was with Him throughout the entire ordeal, from His arrest to His resurrection. He was with Him in the Person of the Holy Spirit, helping Him finish the race (Heb 9:14).

4. "With long life I will satisfy him": It's true that Jesus lived only thirty-three years on earth, which doesn't qualify as *long life*. But the Father has resurrected Him, and now He is alive forevermore, never again to die. The Father is now satisfying Him with long life forever and ever.

Because of resurrection, all aspects of the promises in Psalm 91 have been fulfilled in Christ. The Father has shown His Son His magnificent salvation!

Now let's look at the identificational meaning of the passage and how it applies to our lives. When we're being crucified with Christ, Jesus now speaks over our lives the same fantastic promises the Father spoke over Him. In your trial, hear Jesus now speaking these words over you:

> Because he has set his love upon Me, therefore I will deliver
> him; I will set him on high, because he has known My name. He
> shall call upon Me, and I will answer him; I will be with him in
> trouble; I will deliver him and honor him. With long life I will
> satisfy him, and show him My salvation
> (Ps 91:14-16).

Your trial may be fiery, but look at how you're responding: You're loving the Father just as Jesus did on His cross.

There are some keys that, to handle them, require scars.

You're taking it in your hands and feet; you're drinking the reproach of people; you're wrestling with demons; you're enduring the hiddenness of God; you're standing on the nail and giving Him your love. *Just like Jesus.* This is the identificational nature of the cross.

Can you hear the promises Jesus is making over your life? Because you have set your love on Him, He's promising to deliver you. If He doesn't deliver you in the present moment, it's because He's got an even greater deliverance planned for you. He's going to set you on high because you've come to know His name through your journey. You've been calling on Him, and He promises, "I will answer you!" He assures you that He'll be with you all the way through the trial, and then will deliver and honor you. He will satisfy you with long life—which means that, not only will you live out your full span of allotted years, but they will be *satisfying* years. And to cap off all the goodness, He says that He'll show you the greatness of His salvation. What's it like when God shows you His salvation? You want to find out!

Because you have shared with Christ in His sufferings, you will also share with Him in all the wonderful promises of Psalm 91. Never let go your promises!

Four Places of Comfort

I didn't really connect that much with the cross when I was young and strong. The idea of identifying with Christ in His sufferings didn't seem to have any relevance to my life. But when tragedy hit my life at age thirty-five, I found myself returning over and over to four places in my Bible: Psalms, Job, Lamentations 3, and the cross. I'll mention them briefly.

Psalms. In my trial, I immersed myself in the book of Psalms. I always loved that book, but even more so in tragedy. That's when the promises of Psalm 91 became my survival. I used to think that certain psalms were morbid, such as

Psalm 88, but suddenly I found all the psalms to be powerfully lifegiving. Now, I'm crazy in love with the book of Psalms! Over and over, they express the cry of my heart as I call on Him to fulfill His promises.

The book of Job also became a lifeline for me. I always had a fascination with that book, but in the face of trauma, it ministered to me in profound ways. Job's story shows how God infuses divine purpose into the tragedies of life and redeems what the enemy meant for evil so that, by the time the story is done, the enemy regrets his decision to take you on. Job's story continues to strengthen my resolve to wait on God for His visitation.

I was also drawn to Lamentations 3. The whole book of Lamentations is awesome, but I've connected especially with the third chapter because that's where Jeremiah verbally processed his own personal pain in Jerusalem's destruction. I've become a friend of Lamentations 3.

In my fiery trial, the cross is the fourth place in Scripture to which my heart has been drawn. When deep darkness hit my life, suddenly the cross became my lifeline. When I saw that our sufferings are an identification with Christ's sufferings to a certain extent, suffering was infused with dignity and purpose. The cross provided the lens I needed to comprehend how God was fathering me. Without the cross, I would have lost my mind.

When you're in an agonizing trial, I recommend that you spend much time in these four passages: Lamentations 3, the book of Job, the cross, and Psalms. They'll help you understand the identificational nature of the cross.

Let's stay with this theme and examine the identificational sufferings of the cross as seen in Psalm 74. Come to the next chapter!

He died with the voice of a Lamb (Luke 23:46) and resurrected with the voice of a Lion (Rev 1:15).

For Group Study and Discussion

1. "Always be ready to pray, always be ready to preach, and always be ready to die." How does that statement from John Wesley inspire you?

2. In your Bible reading this week, look for a verse you can place over the cross to find new meaning. Share the verse with the group, and what it means to you.

3. To what extent do you feel you've partaken of Christ's sufferings? (1 Pet 4:13). Were you suffering according to God's will? Tell us about it.

4. *Endure the discipline, embrace the promise.* Do you resonate with that dictum? If so, tell us how it speaks to your life.

5. In suffering, the author was drawn to Lamentations 3, the book of Job, the cross, and Psalms. How about you? What portions of Scripture have been helpful to you in suffering?

6. As you close, let your prayers be guided by Psalm 91:14-16.

CHAPTER THIRTEEN

"If You Love Me So Much, Why Am I in So Much Pain?"

Psalm 74 is a lament, and it's rarely talked about by preachers and teachers because of its mournful tone— mourning the desolations of Jerusalem at the hand of Babylon. The writer, Asaph, seemed to foresee the time that Babylon would invade Jerusalem, burn the temple, level the city, kill many of the people, and take most of the survivors captive to Babylon. Jerusalem's sufferings would be severe, and Psalm 74 personified and portrayed the anguish. Here are the first ten verses:

Ps 74:1 O God, why have You cast us off forever? Why does Your anger smoke against the sheep of Your pasture? 2 Remember Your congregation, which You have purchased of old, the tribe of Your inheritance, which You have redeemed— this Mount Zion where You have dwelt. 3 Lift up Your feet to the perpetual desolations. The enemy has damaged everything in the sanctuary. 4 Your enemies roar in the midst of Your meeting place; they set up their banners for signs. 5 They seem like men who lift up axes among the thick trees. 6 And now they break down its carved work, all at once, with axes and hammers. 7 They have set fire to Your sanctuary; they have defiled the dwelling place of Your name to the ground. 8 They said in their hearts, "Let us destroy them altogether." They have burned up all the meeting places of God in the land. 9 We do not see our signs; there is no longer any prophet; nor is there any among us who knows how long. 10 O God, how long will the adversary reproach? Will the enemy blaspheme Your name forever?

Jerusalem suffered at the hand of Babylon in ways that many of us also suffer in our adversities:

What kind of Man looks at the crushing He's about to undergo and gives thanks? (Luke 22:19).

- We're cast off (v. 1).
- Our desolations are perpetual—never ending—and beyond recovery (v. 3).
- We're hewn down, as men level trees with axes (v. 5).
- We see no sign of anything changing, and the spiritual leaders we usually consult in tough times have no answers for us, nor do they know how long these troubles will last (v. 9).
- We're under reproach from our neighbors, and God's name is blasphemed (v. 10).

In the midst of such dire distress, the psalmist went on to make this statement: "Oh, do not deliver the life of Your turtledove to the wild beast!" (Ps 74:19). Even though he was suffering intensely, he said to the Lord, *I'm Your turtledove.* He was speaking of how precious he knew he was to God.

The psalmist was torn between conflicting realities. Everything in his world had been made desolate; but on the other hand, he felt the Lord's affections in a sweet and personal way. How could he be suffering so intensely while at the same time feeling the Lord's pleasure so clearly? He didn't know how to reconcile the mixed signals of both intimacy and forsakenness, of both delight and dread. He was God's hurting turtledove.

Turtledove. It's stunning that one of the sweetest metaphors of relationship with Jesus in the whole Bible is given in the context of intense suffering. Suffering and intimacy kiss at the cross.

Suffering has the amazing potential of awakening us to intimacy. Why is that so? Well, for starters, pain presses us into God. When we're in a state of perpetual desolations, we become desperate for God. Desperation makes us hungry and thirsty for the fullness of the kingdom of God, and that hunger drives us into God (Prov 16:26). In our desperation to touch answered prayer, we experience the benefits of drawing close to God (Matt 5:6).

Pursuing God while in pain is altogether life-transforming. Here are some of the changes you'll experience:

- Your prayer life will grow stronger.
- You'll experience a dimension of intimacy you never knew before the desolations.
- Your knowledge of God and His ways will increase.
- Your understanding of Scripture will deepen.
- Your character will be refined and purified.
- You'll become a partaker of His holiness (Heb 12:10).
- Your compassion for hurting people will enlarge.
- You'll develop greater sensitivity to hear His voice and perceive His activities in the earth.
- You'll gain spiritual authority with heaven, people, and demons.

Suffering with Christ is a doorway to the high hills of the kingdom. You're cast off, forsaken, hewn down, and abandoned, and yet you feel closer to Him than ever. You're wracked with pain, and yet you love Him more than ever.

You can't help but wonder, *God, if You love me so much, why am I in so much pain?* You're curled in a fetal position, trying to process the pain, and just when you think your life is over, He draws near and whispers, "You're My turtledove."

"I long to believe that I'm Your turtledove, Lord, but if it's true, wouldn't You stop the pain?" I wonder if Jesus had questions like that while on the cross. There's a time, on the cross, when some of the deepest questions of the soul receive no answer and all you hear is, "You're My turtledove. I love you."

This is how the Father felt about Jesus on the cross, and now this is how He feels about you. It's the identificational nature of the cross.

> When God plans a crucifixion, He always plans a resurrection.

My Turtledove Story

Turtledoves are beautiful birds with their silvery-gray feathers and dark, lovely eyes. They live in almost every country on earth, feed mostly on grass seeds, and are almost always seen in pairs because of their loyalty in love: They mate for life. They're inseparable lovebirds!

One day in my youth, I was driving down the highway, doing around fifty miles per hour, when I looked ahead and saw a couple turtledoves waddling out onto the road.

Now, I was trained by my driving tutors to never swerve for animals. They told me stories about people who swerved their car to miss a cat or dog and ended up hitting another vehicle or a person. They convinced me to never swerve for an animal, but only for people.

So when I saw the turtledoves walking onto the road in their search for seeds, I said to them, "You better move. I don't swerve." But they kept moving out into the roadway. By the time they saw me, they tried to escape but it was too late. I hit them both at fifty miles per hour. A cloud of feathers filled the sky behind me. As I drove away, I thought to myself, *Those birds should have moved out of the way.*

It was later that I learned something about turtledoves. They get so fixated on one another and their search for seeds that it's almost as though they have tunnel vision. They lose their peripheral awareness. The lovebirds were so distracted with each other that they didn't even see me coming—until it was too late.

That's what we're like with Jesus. We're totally distracted by Him. We're turtledoves who do everything together and just can't keep our eyes off each other.

While you're on this cross, He'll say things to you that will intoxicate you with His affections: "You're My darling, My beloved, My favorite, the apple of My eye. I'm right here, always with you. I'm for you. We're building a storyline together. Let's do meals together. Let's do mornings together, afternoons together. Let's do evenings together. Let's do people together. Let's do life together."

You're like, "Why haven't I been able to see, until now, that I'm Your turtledove?"

His answer is like, "When things were going great for you and life was comfortable, it wasn't this passionate between us. You were so distracted, so chill. You were satisfied with our relationship. You didn't really seem to need Me that much. But now that you're on this cross, look at you! What zeal! What fervency! You have doves eyes, My love. You never used to chase Me like this, not until the desolations. But now that you're hewn down and under reproach, you can't get your eyes off Me. Turn your eyes away from Me, for they overwhelm Me!"

Jesus drank this cup when on His cross, and now you're drinking the same cup on your cross. Look at the two of you—inseparable in life, in suffering, in death, and in resurrection.

Speaking of the cup of suffering, the Lord's Supper is a beautiful celebration of our identificational sufferings with Christ. When He gives us His broken body to eat, we also give Him our bodies—which means we pledge Him our strength, time, energy, and even our very flesh. And when He gives us His blood to drink, we also pledge our blood to Him, even if it means the shedding of our own blood. We drink the cup to show Him we don't love our lives even unto death (Rev 12:11). This table celebrates that we withhold from each other *nothing*.

I'm speaking of the identificational nature of the cross. Give me another chapter to try to do justice to such a sublime topic.

Small cross small resurrection. Perhaps that's why your trial is so intense.

For Group Study and Discussion

1. Many Psalms are laments. What role has lament had in your prayer life? When you mourn, how have you experienced the Lord's comfort?

2. In the midst of suffering, has the Lord called you His turtledove, or expressed strong pleasure in your devotion? Tell us of your experience. In what ways do you connect with the title of this chapter?

3. Do an online study of turtledoves, and bring your findings to the group. Explain what you found interesting in your research.

4. Read Psalm 74 carefully, and pick some verses to study in a focused way. Share with the group the parts of the psalm that have meant the most to you.

5. As you close, pray with Psalm 74 open before you. Anyone can offer a prayer from the verse of their choosing.

CHAPTER FOURTEEN
David's Greatest Honor

The greatest honor in David's life was not that he wrote many of the Bible's psalms. The greatest honor in his life was not that he was king of Israel, or that he was given an everlasting throne.

The greatest honor in David's life was being quoted three times on the cross.

"My God, My God, why have You forsaken Me?" (Ps 22:1).

"I thirst!" (Ps 143:6).

"Into Your hand I commit my spirit" (Ps 31:5).

When Jesus was in the throes of His agony and looking for language to express the angst of His soul, He reached back to David. He was like, "David said it the way I feel it right now."

David, I need to ask you a question. What kind of a journey would you have to walk in order to write the kind of thing Jesus would *want* to quote on the cross?

David might answer, "I was cast off, perpetually desolate, hewn down, under reproach, with no sign of anything changing and no one knew how long it would go on like this. It was there, in that season, that I wrote the things Jesus quoted on the cross."

David probably couldn't figure out why his crucible was so intense. He must have wondered, *Why does the fire never stop? Why are my pain levels so intense? Why is it that I alone, among all my peers, hurt like this? God, why is my suffering incessant and agonizing?*

At the time, David couldn't make sense of the intensity of his trials. But when Jesus was on the cross, everything must have come into focus for him. I imagine him thinking, So *THIS is why it hurt so badly! My sufferings enabled me to write things that Jesus could quote on the cross.*

I believe in the cross because it offers a God-sized gospel.

At the cross, David's sufferings took on a dignity he couldn't have possibly anticipated.

When we get to the Marriage Supper of the Lamb and we're all seated at the table, visiting with one another about the things of the kingdom, there's only one person among all of heaven's hosts who will be able to say, "He quoted me three times on the cross."

Think about the affinity David must feel with Jesus over this. Because that's what the whole thing was about: identificational suffering and one-of-a-kind intimacy. Jesus wants to have the same kind of affinity with us, too. Our flesh might recoil from such suffering in the moment, but a day is coming when we'll have clarity on His holy purposes.

David, you thought you were cast off, hewn down, desolate and forsaken; but, in fact, now you enjoy with Jesus a knowing relationship of unique significance. Your flesh scrambled to avoid this, but now you appreciate the Father's perfect leadership in your life. Suffering was your portal to the highest intimacy.

This helps me understand why the God I love and serve crushes His favorites. This helps me understand His fathering paradigm. It's all an invitation to the identificational nature of the cross.

No angel gets a cross. The cross is an honor too high for angels. No angel gets a cross, and no angel gets a resurrection. But you? You get both. It's your highest dignity.

Suffering Matures Us

God uses suffering to mature and prepare us for the Marriage Supper of the Lamb. I can suppose Jesus thinking, *I didn't suffer like that on the cross so that I could marry a spoiled, entitled brat.*

Jesus doesn't want to marry a bride who, on the wedding night, gets out a bunch of play dolls, and then pouts in a corner while sucking her thumb. He died to gain for Himself an equally yoked, co-equal partner with whom He'll rule the universe forever.

How will He gain such a partner? By giving her the same cup He Himself drank. Adversity will be her way forward into full bridal maturity.

When we're finally joined to Jesus fully and completely at the Marriage Supper of the Lamb, let me suggest what the conversation will *not* sound like. The bride will *not* be saying things like, "Jesus, this is our wedding day, a time of happiness and joy. Let's not talk about the cross right now. You know, I never really did connect with that part of Your story. It always struck me as gruesome and morbid. To bring it up now would be a downer, and I want us to enjoy this moment. Can we just not go there right now, but enjoy the brightness of this cheerful moment?"

I think the conversation might more closely resemble something like this:

He: "Let Me tell you about Abba's will for My life."

She: "I also want to talk to You about the Father's will for my life."

He: "I want to talk about the cup the Father gave Me."

She: "The Father also gave me a bitter cup, and I've been waiting to talk to You about it."

He: "When I walked the earth, everything was against Me."

She: "Yeah, everything was against me, too."

He: "I stepped into the battle and came away with scars."

She: "I've always admired that about You. And I incurred some scars myself in the battle."

He: "Here, I want to show you My scars."

She: "Those scars are so precious to me because they brought me Your love. And I also want to show You mine."

If there is no hell, the cross is absurd. If we don't need to be saved from something horrific, then why such a drastic payment?

There's a day coming when I will reach my hand into His side, just like Thomas did in John 20:27, and I will caress the scars that brought me into His embrace.

And then He will reach with His hand, and He will caress the scars of His bride because she also bears in her body the marks of the Lord Jesus (Gal 6:17). Our intimacy in that moment will be based upon our common wounds.

Who would even want to arrive at the Marriage Supper of the Lamb without any scars?

There was a time when the wounds were our reproach. But on that day, He'll dignify the scars as tokens of our intimacy and of our identification in shared sufferings. They'll be badges of honor and emblems of our marriage bed.

Suffering Releases Creatives

Amy Carmichael was a missionary who suffered painfully from physical infirmity. Author of many poems, her identification with Christ's sufferings comes through especially in this gripping piece:

Hast Thou No Scar?

Hast thou no scar?
No hidden scar on foot, or side, or hand?
I hear thee sung as mighty in the land
I hear them hail thy bright ascendant star
Hast thou no scar?

Hast thou no wound?
Yet I was wounded by the archers, spent,
Leaned Me against a tree to die; and rent,
By ravening beasts that encompassed Me, I swooned;
Hast thou no wound?

No wound? No scar?
Yet, as the Master shall the servant be,
And piercéd are the feet that follow Me
But thine are whole: can he have followed far
Who has no wound nor scar?

Suffering released Amy's poetic gift, just as it has for many others. Some of the bride of Christ's best poetry and songs have proceeded from her sufferings. The Psalms are prime examples of that because many of them were birthed in a place of hardship and struggle. The same is also true of our contemporary hymns. When you hear the stories behind the songs we sing—that is, the circumstances in which the song-writers wrote them—you're gripped with the realization that some of our best songs were forged through adversity. Songs birthed in tragedy and hardship have often been among the most helpful, historically through the centuries, in enabling the bride to give her heart to her Lord.

The inverse is also true. When life is happy and circum-stances are comfortable, fewer songs seem to be written, and those that are don't carry the same depth and punch. For a biblical example of that, consider the sixteen months David lived in Ziklag. That was a season of relative serenity for him, and we have no psalms ascribed to his stay in that city. In calm and comfort, new songs waned. It was when adversity intensified that his songwriting blossomed.

Suffering unlocks songwriters. In times of adversity, "Deep calls unto deep at the noise of Your waterfalls" (Ps 42:7). Deep things in us reach for deep things in God. Crucified songwriters supply some of the sweetest songs for the bride of Christ because they're experiencing the identificational nature of the cross.

Jesus Created the Human Body for Crucifixion

Jesus created the human body to experience maximum suffering during crucifixion.

When the Trinity partnered together at creation to fash-ion the human body, Jesus knew He was forming a body that He Himself would inhabit for thirty-three years on earth, and then forever.

History's greatest race was run by a Man with His feet nailed to a tree.

The following conversation is fictional because it didn't actually happen, but my holy imagination wonders if, during the creation process, the Father might have said something like this to Jesus: "Son, are You sure You want to put all those nerve endings in the hands and feet like that? That's where they're going to put the nails!"

I suppose the Son possibly answering something like this: "Yes, Abba, I know. I want to put those nerves there because I want to connect implicitly with their sorrows and feel them all the way through my entire being."

Nobody has suffered like God. He has drunk more deeply of sorrow and agony than any human being. Now, nobody can look at the cross and say, "You have no idea what it's like to suffer the way I do. You don't understand *my* world of pain." The sufferings of the cross were so intense that now Jesus empathizes implicitly with the pain of the person living in the lowest hell hole. At the cross, God suffered more than anyone and everyone so that He could reach anyone and everyone.

Would you like to know how Jesus feels about you? He feels about you in His scalp, His temples, His cheeks, His eyes, His neck, His shoulders, His arms, His wrists, His hands, His chest, His back, His abdomen, His loins, His thighs, His knees, His calves, His ankles, and His feet. He feels about you from the follicles of His head to the ends of His toes. Love for you runs the entire course of His being.

What's a fitting way for me to respond to such love? Surely He deserves more than just a 45-degree elbow bend in a Sunday morning worship service. He deserves a love that bursts from every molecule of my being!

Jesus, I love You with my head, my hair, my ears, my eyes, my tongue, my neck, my shoulders, my arms, my hands, my torso, my loins, my legs, and my feet. Jesus, I love You with all my body, soul, heart, mind, and strength.

He Withholds Nothing from Me

Whenever I'm suffering, I go back to the cross. When I don't know how to process the difficulties in my journey, I just go back to the cross. When I can't see my way forward, I go back to the cross. When I don't know how to make sense of my pain levels, I go back to the cross.

When I hear that ancient accusation, "He's withholding from you," I just go back to the cross. I hear that accusation from the accuser a lot, actually, because it's one of his most common accusations. That accusation goes all the way back to the garden of Eden when the accuser said to Eve, "God knows that in the day you eat of it your eyes will be opened, and you will be like God, knowing good and evil" (Gen 3:5). The accusation was, "God knows that this fruit would usher you into your destiny, but He's withholding it from you because He doesn't want you to become everything you could be." He used that accusation on Eve, and he's still using it on people today. In fact, it's still one of his favorite accusations against God.

Here's how Satan uses that accusation on me personally. He often says to me things like, "God's withholding from you the healing that would open up and complete your story, purpose, and destiny."

Whenever I hear that ancient accusation, I just go back to the cross because the cross *nails* that accusation. When I look at the cross, I don't see a God who's withholding from me; rather, I see a God who's giving me His *everything*. He's giving me His best—His only begotten Son. On the cross, I see a God who spreads His arms and, with nails in His hands and feet, says to me, "I love you with all My heart, with all My mind, with all My soul, with all My flesh, and with all My strength. I love you with My last breath. I love you with My last drop of blood."

Jesus is our cross-fit trainer, teaching us how to run our race (Heb 12:1-2).

Beholding this love now gives me the courage to stand on *my* nail, spread my arms wide, and say to Him, "I love You with all my heart, with all my soul, with all my mind, and with all my strength. I love You with my time, with my priorities, with my energies, with my gifts and talents, with my treasures, with the words of my mouth, and I do not love my life even unto death. I am Yours and You are mine."

This is the identificational nature of the cross.

I declare in the presence of the angels and all creation that my God withholds *nothing* from me. He's already given me His everything. If He should never give me another benefit for the rest of my days on this earth, He's already given me more than I deserve. He might *restrain* Himself for a while from answering my prayer, but He's not *withholding* the answer from me. And if He is strategically restraining my deliverance for a season, it's because He's got an even stronger story for me than I had for myself.

For Group Study and Discussion

1. Spend a few moments talking about the intimacy and solidarity David must feel with Jesus, after being quoted three times on the cross.

2. Look more closely at the three Davidic quotes. What do those quotes reveal about your own walk with God?

3. *Suffering matures us:* In what ways do you agree or disagree?

4. In what way have you been scarred in the battle? What does it mean to bear in our body the marks of Jesus? (Gal 6:17).

5. Have you ever been tempted to accuse God of withholding Himself from you? How did you walk through that?

6. As you close, let your prayers express to the Lord that you're withholding nothing from Him (Mark 12:30).

CHAPTER FIFTEEN

The Cross in the Book of Job

Some people struggle to find the book of Job instructive and helpful because, when they look at the teachings and miracles of Jesus, they can't find anything in His ministry to correspond to Job's story. For example, Job was struck with boils, but Jesus didn't go around afflicting people with boils or any other kind of sickness; rather, He went around healing everyone who was oppressed by the devil (Acts 10:38). Job's ten children were killed by a tornado, but Jesus never killed anyone's children; quite the contrary, He raised children from the dead.

Because of these differences, some are not able to find Jesus in the book of Job and, therefore, consider the book to be suspect and questionable. But in comparing the book of Job to Jesus' teaching and miracle ministry, I think they've stopped just short. They should have gone a bit further and looked at His cross because, when you do, the similitudes between Job's experience and the cross suddenly infuse remarkable meaning into Job's story.

When the book of Job is viewed in light of Calvary, we realize that his life was the first signpost in Scripture to the cross. What a stunning legacy! I hope I can help you see it.

When Job's story is introduced to us, we are shown a man with ten children, grandchildren (see Job 19:17), and a robust income stream—he was one of the wealthiest people of his day—with houses, lands, possessions, livestock, children, and servants. Furthermore, he was viewed by heaven as the most upright man on earth and consequently enjoyed supernatural protection from harm and danger.

The story took a dramatic turn when Job lost his livestock, his income stream, his servants, and his ten children—all in one day. A bit later, he took a devastating blow to his health. After a lengthy theodical and theological debate with his friends, he experienced a sudden, supernatural reversal that restored his health, wealth, and legacy. The ordeal ended in a redemption story.

How can we see Jesus in such a story? I suggest we view it this way: If Job's early successes correspond to Christ's earthly ministry, and if his trials correspond to Christ's death, then his restoration corresponds to Christ's resurrection.

I invite you to view Job's fiery trial as an identification with the cross of Christ. With that perspective as our lens, I want to suggest some ways to see the cross of Christ in the book of Job.

25 Ways to Find the Cross in the Book of Job

Here are some of the ways we can see Christ and His cross in Job's trials.

1. In the book of Job, the most upright man on earth (Job 1:8) suffered the most of anyone on earth. That certainly reminds me of Christ's cross, where the most upright Man to walk our planet suffered more than any other human being ever has.

2. Trembling with pain in the freshness of his trial, Job cried, "Naked I came from my mother's womb, and naked shall I return there" (Job 1:21). That statement describes Jesus perfectly as He was born naked and then died naked on the tree.

3. Job was so disfigured by his sufferings that his friends didn't recognize him (Job 2:12). In a similar way, when Isaiah prophesied about Christ's execution, he said, "His visage was marred more than any man" (Isa 52:14).

When the launch of Your ministry means crucifixion, You don't mind waiting thirty years.

4. Eliphaz goaded Job to call out to God for help (Job 5:1), insinuating he would receive no reply because of his wickedness. They taunted Christ on the cross with similar words, saying, "He trusted in God; let Him deliver Him now if He will have Him" (Matt 27:43).

5. In speaking of his friends who were attacking him, Job said, "They gape at me with their mouth, they strike me reproachfully on the cheek, they gather together against me" (Job 16:10). This is reminiscent of Christ's sufferings, regarding which David prophetically spoke, "They gape at Me with their mouths" (Ps 22:13). They also struck Jesus on the cheek (Luke 22:64).

6. Job cried out, "O earth, do not cover my blood" (Job 16:18). This reminds us that the earth didn't cover the blood of Jesus at Calvary, either. Instead, His blood continues to testify and speak on our behalf before the throne of God (Heb 12:24).

7. Job bemoaned, "Why do You hide Your face, and regard me as Your enemy?" (Job 13:24). This reminds us of Jesus' cry on the cross, "My God, My God, why have You forsaken Me?" (Matt 27:46). Both Job and Jesus felt forsaken by God, and both of them asked why.

8. When Job needed his friends most, they failed him. The same thing happened to Jesus. At His arrest, His friends "forsook Him and fled" (Matt 26:56).

9. Job wrote, "You set a limit for the soles of my feet" (Job 13:27). That certainly would be true of Christ, whose feet were immobilized by nails.

10. When you consider the causative agents of Job's trial, you realize he was afflicted by God, the devil, and people. That same trilogy of causative agents was behind the cross. Let

me remind you how these three agents worked together to crucify Jesus. People—Jewish leaders arrested Jesus, and Roman soldiers crucified Him. Satan—the devil filled the Jewish leaders with a demonic envy, and he commandeered Judas to betray the Lord. God—"God so loved the world that He gave His only begotten Son" for us (John 3:16). Again, both Job's and Jesus' trials were caused by God, the devil, and people.

11. Job's best friend, Eliphaz, became so frustrated with him that he concocted charges against him (Job 22:6-9). Similarly, Jesus was accused by false witnesses at His trial before the high priest (Mark 14:56).

12. Job was raised up from his sufferings when He interceded for his friends (Job 42:7-10). In a similar sense, Jesus prayed for us on the cross (Isa 53:12) and resurrected as our great Intercessor and High Priest (Heb 7:25-26).

13. When God accepted and received Job, He raised him up (Job 42:9). Similarly, when God accepted Christ's sacrifice, He raised Him up (Rom 4:25).

14. In the bitterness of his soul, Job cried, "He destroys the blameless and the wicked" (Job 9:22). To gain a visual on that statement, look at the three crosses on Golgotha's hill where both the blameless and wicked were crucified and died together.

15. Job and Jesus are both cornerstones. The book of Job was the first book of the Bible put on paper, which means it was the first foundation stone the Holy Spirit planted when He began to erect the edifice we call Holy Scripture. Therefore, we can rightly call the book of Job the cornerstone of Scripture. Jesus is also a cornerstone—He's the cornerstone of the church (Isa 28:16; Acts 4:11). Job

All we could do was crucify Him, He did the rest.

is rejected by some as the cornerstone of Scripture, but I suppose that shouldn't surprise us too much because the builders commonly reject the cornerstone (Ps 118:22).

16. Since Job is the first Bible book written, and since it points to the cross, we rightly conclude (as already stated) that Job's life story is the first signpost in Scripture to the cross.

17. Suffering was a qualifier for both Job and Jesus. For what was Job qualifying through his trial? To write the first book of the Bible, to be the first signpost in Scripture to the cross, to gain a spiritual inheritance in every generation, and to become a great patriarch in the faith. For what was Jesus qualifying in His agonizing death? He qualified to serve as our Redeemer, our High Priest, the Captain of our salvation, and the Apostle of our confession. Suffering qualified both of them for a greater rank in the kingdom of God.

18. Neither Job nor Jesus did anything wrong to incur their sufferings. The Holy Spirit launched Job's story by testifying to his righteousness: "There was a man in the land of Uz, whose name was Job; and that man was blameless and upright, and one who feared God and shunned evil" (Job 1:1). Job's trial, therefore, was not the consequence of sin in his life. In the same way, Jesus was crucified even though He had done nothing wrong. He was the sinless, blameless Lamb of God (1 Pet 1:19).

19. Job spoke of his sufferings as labor (Job 9:29). Christ's sufferings were also called labor, for He labored on the cross to obtain our salvation (Isa 53:11).

20. People suffer a wide gamut of afflictions in this world, and for all of them to receive consolation from Job's example, he had to suffer in literally every major area of life. He suffered in his marriage, family, relationships, finances,

livelihood, and physical health. Because of that, his life story is a meaningful and helpful witness to people who suffer almost any kind of adversity in this life. In the same way, Jesus suffered in every manner imaginable so that He can save, deliver, and heal people who suffer in any manner whatsoever.

21. Both Job and Jesus suffered in the will of God (1 Pet 4:19). We know it was God's will for Job to suffer because God, not Satan, picked the fight and initiated the whole ordeal. We also know it was God's will for Jesus to suffer on the cross so He could redeem us to God (Rev 14:4).

22. God didn't spare either Job or Jesus from deep suffering. Job said, "He did not hide deep darkness from my face" (Job 23:17). And Scripture said of the Father that He "did not spare His own Son" (Rom 8:32).

23. Job wished that he had a mediator to represent him to God: "Nor is there any mediator between us, who may lay his hand on us both" (Job 9:33). The cross provided for us precisely the mediator that Job desired. Through His intercession on the cross, Christ became our Mediator to God. Paul testified of this: "For there is one God and one Mediator between God and men, the Man Christ Jesus" (1 Tim 2:5). Thank God, we now have a Mediator!

24. Job cried, "Though He slay me, yet will I trust Him" (Job 13:15). Jesus displayed this same trust on the cross. He trusted His Father even while He was slaying Him. With His last breath Jesus prayed, "'Father, into Your hands I commit My spirit.' Having said this, He breathed His last" (Luke 23:46).

25. Although there are doubtless many more ways to see Jesus in the book of Job, I close this chapter with this

Sometimes they've got to crucify their leader before they know what they've got.

final thought. I believe it was Jesus Himself who spoke with Job at the end of his trial (Job 38-42). We're told that God answered Job out of a whirlwind (Job 38:1). We're also told that He showed Himself visibly to Job, for Job testified, "I have heard of You by the hearing of the ear, but now my eye sees You" (Job 42:5). Job saw God with his eyes! However, John wrote, "No one has seen God at any time" (John 1:18; 1 John 4:12). John meant that no one has ever seen the Father at any time. But quite a few people in the Bible saw the Son of God—before, during, and after His incarnation. It seems, therefore, that Job didn't see the Father but the Son. Job both saw Jesus with his eyes and heard His voice with his ears. I'm suggesting it was Jesus Himself who interrogated and exonerated Job in chapters 38-42. For me, therefore, the presence of Jesus in the book of Job is unmistakable, undeniable, and altogether wonderful.

Some have supposed that the cross rendered the book of Job obsolete and no longer relevant to our lives. To the contrary, the cross confirmed the glory of Job's story and emphasized its relevance for new covenant believers because he participated so undeniably in *the identificational nature of the cross.*

With this chapter in the quiver of your understanding, I hope that every time you read the book of Job you'll be able to see more and more of Jesus in that marvelous cornerstone of Scripture.

For Group Study and Discussion

1. Read John 18-20 this week, and share with the group what moved you most in this reading of the crucifixion account.

2. If you've ever struggled to see Jesus in the book of Job, explain your struggle. How has it helped you to view the book of Job as an excursus on the cross?

3. Of the 25 ways listed in this chapter, choose one to study more deeply on your own, and share your discoveries at our next meeting.

4. Of the 25 ways listed, which one was most surprising or revelational to you?

5. Can you find something else about Jesus and the cross, in the book of Job, that wasn't mentioned in this chapter? Share it with the group.

6. Is there a specific way this chapter has helped you in your walk? If so, tell us about it.

7. As you close, express prayers that center around Job 19:23-27.

The Labor of the Cross

What would it look like if God were to use all His strength to come and save you? To find your answer, look at Calvary. The cross was a holy construction site—*God at work*—where He labored with all His strength to accomplish something of gargantuan proportions for us.

Jesus also worked strenuously at Calvary's construction site. He labored with all His heart, soul, body, and mind; He agonized with blood, sweat, and tears. He used all His strength to absorb the punishment for sin and earn our salvation. Isaiah called the cross a labor of love when he prophesied that the Father would look upon Jesus, "see the *labor* of His soul, and be satisfied" (Isa 53:11).

After Jesus finished the job, the Father conducted a post-construction inspection. He visited the site, examined the work, stamped it with His approving imprimatur, and raised up His Son. "Excellent. You did it. Job well done. You finished the thing." The Father didn't resurrect Jesus merely to get Him out of a tight spot, but to demonstrate He had successfully executed His assignment.

At the cross, He did the hard work; at the resurrection, He collected the paycheck.

Calvary was the marathon; resurrection was the awards ceremony.

Your Tomb Is a Womb

The cross was a *womb*. During His sufferings Jesus was in labor, and at the resurrection He celebrated the birth. Jesus said so when He spoke of the cross as childbirth: "A woman, when she is in labor, has sorrow because her hour has come; but as soon as she has given birth to the child, she no longer remembers the anguish, for joy that a human being has been born into the world" (John 16:21). On the cross, Jesus was laboring to birth the redemption of humanity. When He had completed His assignment, He resurrected and said, "Rejoice!" because the church was born (Matt 28:9).

Just as it was for Jesus, your tomb is a womb. He redeems that which feels like a death sentence and turns it into new life. When you're in a fiery trial, you're actually experiencing birth pangs. You've been gestating something for a long time, and now you're in hard labor. If it feels like you're giving birth to something, it's because you are!

Are you in a fiery trial? Are you identifying with the cross? Then get ready for hard work, because nothing great is birthed without hard labor. You'll work hard in your soul, mind, body, and spirit to lay hold of His purpose in your adversities. You'll travail in the word, in fasting, and in prayer to keep a tight hold on your promises. You'll strive to preserve faith, to guard your holiness, to buy the gold of Christlikeness (Rev 3:18), and to keep yourself in the love of God (Jude 1:21).

Everyone who looked at the cross thought it was a massive setback, and you'll probably feel the same way about your trial. The whole ordeal will feel like a huge setback in your life. But God redeems the setbacks of life and turns tombs into wombs. In fact, *nothing* advances in the kingdom of God without an initial setback. For the ultimate example, look at the cross.

How can we endure in labor until the baby is birthed? By "looking unto Jesus" (Heb 12:2). His example will enable you to travail in your trial, and His resurrection will assure you that your resurrection is coming, too. God is going to birth something through your trial that will be so glorious you'll forget all the sorrow of your birth pangs.

Therefore, get in the Spirit and *push*! Persevere in labor until the thing is birthed. That's what Jesus did. He labored on the cross until He could say, "It is finished."

Resurrection is the Father's validation of the Son's redemptive death.

Of the many things Jesus worked to accomplished, He labored to qualify for a higher rank in the kingdom of God. Let's look at that.

Jesus Qualified for a Higher Rank

The cross was a qualifying meet. Jesus labored on the cross to qualify for a higher rank and office in the kingdom.

Now, we realize that prior to the cross He already held many offices. What were some of those offices? Here's a sampling: He was Lord of heaven and earth, King of kings, Lord of lords, King of the Jews, the Almighty, Alpha and Omega, Chief Shepherd, Commander of heaven's armies, Emmanuel, Light of the world, Messiah, and the Word of God.

But at the cross He was reaching for more. In spite of all the glorious offices He held, there were some functions and ministries He couldn't fulfill until He had completed the labor of the cross. He wanted to save the whole world, but to gain that rank He had to earn His stripes, drink the cup, go the distance, run the race, and finish the course. In other words, He had to *qualify* for that rank.

And He did it! By laboring through an agonizing death, He qualified to serve as our Redeemer, our High Priest, the Captain of our salvation, the Apostle of our confession, the firstborn from the dead, and the Savior of the world.

Now that He has qualified to serve as our High Priest, we cry, "Worthy is the Lamb that was slain!" When we cry *Worthy*, we mean *Qualified*. Through His sufferings, the Lamb of God qualified to take away the sins of the world. Because He completed the labor of the cross, He's now qualified, worthy, and deserving of all our praise!

Qualifying for a greater rank or higher office always takes a whole lot of hard work. For example, if you want to get a degree such as a bachelor's, or master's, or a Ph.D., steel yourself because they're going to work you to death. There's only one way to earn that degree, and that's by putting your nose to the grindstone.

Not all careers require a qualifying process, but here are some that do: lawyer, cop, doctor, nurse, psychologist, dentist, EMT, air traffic controller, firefighter, building inspector, or truck driver. In each of these careers, you won't be allowed to work in the field until you've first done the required grunt work and earned your certification.

On the cross, Jesus labored for His certification as the Captain of our salvation.

Let's look at a couple other heroes of faith who labored for a higher rank in the army of God.

Job and Caleb

Today we view Job as a general in the army of God, but to gain that rank he had to earn his stripes. His trial was a qualifying meet. He endured in faith and eventually qualified for a higher rank in the kingdom. We love his story because he passed the test.

Someone might wonder, "For what did Job qualify?" Here are some of his distinctions: He became the first signpost in Scripture to the cross, he wrote the first book of the Bible, his story became the cornerstone of all Scripture, he gained a spiritual inheritance in every generation, he became a father in the faith and—best of all—he saw God with his own two eyes. I'd say it's appropriate to call him General Job. By enduring through the hard work of his sufferings, he qualified to inspire sufferers of every generation.

Look at all the ways he now inspires believers. If you struggle in your marriage, he'll comfort and help you. If you've lost a child, you can go to Job. If your friends reject you, you'll find that Job understands. If you suffer complete financial ruin, Job

One million years from now, when you see God's holiness clearer than ever, you'll be stunned at the power of the blood to bring you into such holiness.

will talk to you about that, too. If you incur a physical infirmity that nearly takes your life, Job can help you with that, as well. Through his trial, General Job gained the authority to speak to a vast array of difficulties, and that's what has made him a true patriarch of faith.

Caleb was another man in the Bible who qualified for something higher through his trial. What was his trial? He had to wander in the wilderness for forty years with his fellow Israelites. Staying in faith during those forty years was the hardest work of his life! He labored to hold onto his promise that God would bring him through and give him a mountain in the Promised Land. His wilderness was a qualifying meet. He was qualifying for the spiritual authority to take a mountain in Canaan. He was buying spiritual authority in the wilderness—both with the people and God—to ask for and to take an entire mountain. The reason his wilderness lasted so long was because he was buying authority. By the time he had endured in faith for forty years, nobody complained when Joshua allotted him a mountain. Why? Because he had done the time in the wilderness.

There are some spheres of authority for which you must do the time.

All of this applies to your fiery trial.

Your Trial Is a Qualifier

Sometimes the trials we endure are intended by God to qualify us for a higher office. There are some ranks and stations in the kingdom of God for which we must qualify.

View your cross as a qualifying meet. God's not merely punishing or purifying you, He's qualifying you for a higher rank so that you can lay your life down in greater abandonment and selfless servanthood.[1] More than ever, we need generals, lieutenants, and captains in the body of Christ who have

---

1 I explore this theme in my book, *The Chastening of the Lord: The Forgotten Doctrine.*

come through a great crucifixion and have qualified to serve the body of Christ in the last days.

This may help explain why your trial is so intense. Qualifying for high office is always extremely rigorous. If it weren't so difficult, more would occupy those offices.

For Jesus, it meant the cross; for Job, it meant crushing losses; for Caleb, it meant a forty-year wilderness. To earn their stripes, they had to endure in faith. *Endurance*. It's a huge word. Let's talk about it.

Endurance Makes Us Perfect and Complete

Endurance was possibly the most significant virtue on display at Christ's cross (Heb 12:2). The great issue in the balance was, could He endure to the very end until the job was finished? The only way to overcome the cross was through *endurance*.

The same is true for us. The only way we'll overcome in our fiery trials and attain to a higher rank is through endurance.

We don't cope, we endure. There's a huge difference between the two. The world *copes* with their tragedies because they have no way to escape the grip of darkness; but believers *endure* in faith because we have the promise of overcoming. This is why we keep laboring, toiling, reaching, pressing—so that we might prevail just like Jesus. By enduring on the cross in holiness, Jesus prevailed to open the scroll of the Father's destiny for the age to come (Rev 5:5). And now He says to you, "To him who overcomes I will grant to sit with Me on My throne, as I also overcame and sat down with My Father on His throne" (Rev 3:21).

The key ingredient to overcoming is *endurance*. The ancients called it "The Queen of Virtues." For example, St. Nilus of Ancyra wrote:

> The cross is your tree of life. Eat and live.

"This is the queen of virtues, the foundation of virtue, a haven of tranquility. It is peace in time of war, calm in rough waters, safety amidst treachery and danger. It makes those who practice it stronger than steel. No weapons or brandished bows, no turbulent troops or advancing siege engines, no flying spears or arrows can shake it. Not even the host of evil spirits, not the dark array of hostile powers, nor the devil himself standing by with all his armies and devices will have power to injure the man or woman who has acquired this virtue through Christ."[2]

In the following passage, James seemed to support the idea that endurance is the queen of virtues:

My brethren, count it all joy when you fall into various trials, knowing that the testing of your faith produces endurance. But let endurance have its perfect work, that you may be perfect and complete, lacking nothing (James 1:2-4).

"Count it all joy when you fall into various trials" (James 1:2). I consider that to be the most challenging verse in the entire Bible. Why? Because the term *various trials* can include virtually *anything*—even the most terrible of circumstances. Count it all joy when your spouse gets cancer. Count it all joy when your child is in a car accident and hanging on for their life. Count it all joy when your house goes into foreclosure. Count it all joy when you lose your career and must declare bankruptcy. Count it all joy when your spouse divorces you. Count it all joy when you have a heart attack. Count it all joy when a car accident renders you quadriplegic and blind.

If the verse had said, "Count it all depression," I would have known how to do that. But how are we to count it all *joy* when we suffer devastating losses?

The first key is in *knowing* (James 1:3). James said we

2   St. Nilus of Ancrya, "Endurance is the queen of virtues, the foundation of virtue, a heaven of tranquility," Eclectic Orthodoxy, https://afkimel. wordpress.com/2019/11/16/endurance-is-the-queen-of-virtues-the-foundation-of-virtue-a-haven-of-tranquility

need to *know* something. The only way to be joyful in trials is through divine understanding. We need to know God's purpose in trials.

In the 1960s, a quartet-era song had this lyric: "I don't need to understand, I just need to hold His hand." That line rhymed nicely, and the tune was pleasant, but it's just not true. Without understanding, we end up buried by depression. To count it all joy, we must know and understand some things.

Jesus was able to endure the cross because He *knew* something: "By His knowledge My righteous Servant shall justify many, for He shall bear their iniquities" (Isa 53:11). When You're impaled to a cross, You better know something! What did Jesus know? He knew the fickle anger of man, the rage of Satan, and the Father's purpose to redeem humanity. He knew He was bearing the iniquities of the whole world. Knowledge got Him through. When suffering, therefore, pursue knowledge.

What do we need to know? James answered that in verse 3: "knowing that the testing of your faith produces endurance." We need to know that God is using the trial to produce *endurance* in our lives.

In the Greek language, faith is a masculine noun and endurance is a feminine noun. When faith and endurance come together, eventually they give birth to realized promises.

What is endurance? I get my definition from James 1:3-4. *Endurance is faith sustained over time, in the face of adversity.* Latch onto that definition because it's the essence of biblical endurance. Endurance stays in faith over the long haul by holding firmly to His word, even in the face of devastating loss and suffering. Jesus *endured* on the cross, and this is also what you must do in your trial.

James went on to describe what the queen of virtues produces in our lives:

Just as Jesus broke bread to feed a multitude, the Father broke Jesus to feed a planet.

"But let endurance have its perfect work, that you may be perfect and complete, lacking nothing" (James 1:4).

Endurance is the most transformative grace of all Christian virtues. It can change you in ways nothing else can. When we endure—that is, stay in faith in the midst of suffering—we're on a path with God that leads to "perfect and complete, lacking nothing." Said succinctly, endurance has the power to make you perfect and complete. That's what you need to know to count it all joy.

When you endure in faith through fiery trials, you have the potential to come through the trial perfect in knowledge, perfect in the fruit of the Spirit, complete in the gifts of the Spirit, perfect in faith and power, perfect in servanthood and humility, perfect in righteousness and holiness—lacking nothing of the fullness of God.

Your trial isn't a tomb, it's a womb.

No wonder they called endurance the queen of virtues. This makes James 1:4 the fattest promise on the Bible! If James 1:2 is the toughest verse in the Bible, James 1:4 is the biggest promise in the Bible: "that you may be perfect and complete, lacking nothing." Your trial is meant by God to bring you into the perfection of Christ. Therefore, *count it all joy!*

Jesus finished the labor of the cross through endurance, and we'll overcome in our trial the same way. Do whatever it takes to stay in faith!

Our next chapter continues to look at the labor of the cross.

For Group Study and Discussion

1. *On the cross, Jesus earned our salvation. When we try to earn our salvation, we insult His work.* Talk about this truth and what it means to you.

2. Is there a sentence in this chapter that stood out to you, and that you'd like to talk about?

3. Talk about the cross as a womb (John 16:21). How is it helpful to you to view your trial as a womb?

4. *We share in Christ's sufferings so we might qualify for a higher rank in the kingdom.* Is there any way in which you relate to this truth personally?

5. Study the life of Caleb this week. In what way does his example inspire you to go after your own mountain?

6. Do you think endurance is rightly called the queen of virtues? Talk about the author's definition: *Endurance is faith sustained over time, in the face of adversity.*

7. As you close, let James 1:2-4 inform your prayers.

CHAPTER SEVENTEEN

A Mountain Became a Plain

Jesus labored on the cross until God turned the mountain of Calvary into a plain. When I speak of Calvary as a mountain and then a plain, I'm drawing on a metaphor found in a vision that God gave the prophet Zechariah. In the vision, Zechariah saw God turning a mountain into a plain. We're going to look at the original context of his vision, see how it connects with the cross, and then make the metaphor relevant to your journey in God.

As we look at Zechariah's prophecy, you'll be encouraged to labor in your trial until God levels your mountain and turns it into a fruitful plain.

Zerubbabel's Mountain

Zechariah's vision was meant to strengthen the heart of Zerubbabel, the governor of Israel. After their seventy-year exile in Babylon, Zerubbabel led some of Zion's captives back to the land of Israel. Once back in the land, Zerubbabel had a huge mountain in front of him. What was it? A building project. He was called by the Lord to mobilize the labors of the surviving remnant that had returned to Israel, and rebuild God's temple in Jerusalem.

The building project seemed so impossible to Zerubbabel that it loomed before him like an insurmountable mountain. Rebuilding the temple would require a prodigious amount of human labor, a lot of building materials, and strong financial assets—resources that Zerubbabel simply didn't have.

God raised up the prophet Zechariah to encourage Zerubbabel and the people of Israel to devote themselves to the building project. God gave Zechariah several visions that were designed to bolster the courage and resolve of the builders. God knew that, for the people to complete the task before them, they would need prophets to encourage them with the word of the Lord.

Zechariah assured the people that God was with them and it was time to build the temple. His visions and prophecies really encouraged Zerubbabel and the people of Israel, so they gathered their strength and made a final push to complete the temple.

In one of his visions, Zechariah saw God speaking to the looming building project. Here's what God said to it:

> "Who are you, O great mountain? Before Zerubbabel you shall become a plain! And he shall bring forth the capstone with shouts of 'Grace, grace to it!'" (Zech 4:7).

The "great mountain" was the temple building project, and the "plain" was the completion of the building. God declared that the temple would be finished, and when the last stone of the structure was put in place, they would lift up shouts of joy.

The Mountain Is a Who

The words "great mountain" in our verse are a metaphor for an obstacle that looms so large it appears to be unconquerable and unclimbable. God asked of that mountain, "Who are you?" He didn't ask what but who, because the mountain was more than a *what*, it was a *who*. Great mountains always have names. Everest, Matterhorn, Kilimanjaro, Pike's Peak, Rainier—every great mountain is identified with a name.

When you face a great challenge in life, you can probably put a name on your mountain. *Poverty. Infirmity. Bankruptcy. Hatred. Divorce. Loneliness.* Mountains take on a persona or identity of their own. That's because your mountain is a *who*.

One reason the mountains or challenges of life often take on a persona is because they're sometimes empowered by demonic energy. Sometimes a demon with a specific name is assigned to your mountain. The warfare can become so personal that the enemy is no longer a what but a

> Crucifixion is only a chapter in your story. It's not finished until there's resurrection.

who. In spiritual warfare, we look beyond the *what* of natural circumstances to the *who* of evil powers, for "we do not wrestle against flesh and blood, but against principalities, against powers, against the rulers of the darkness of this age, against spiritual hosts of wickedness in the heavenly places" (Eph 6:12).

When God said, "Who are you, O great mountain?", He called Zerubbabel's building project *great*. But He was being sarcastic. To Zerubbabel's eyes, the mountain appeared to be great. In God's eyes, however, it was anything but great. By calling it *great*, therefore, God was poking at it disdainfully. He was scorning and despising the mountain that dared stand and resist His will.

God looks at your trial in the same way. Like He did in 2 Kings 3:18, God looks at the obstacle in your way and thinks to Himself, *You think you're something? You're a light thing in My eyes. Who do you think you are, anyway?* God despises your impossibility!

Desolate Versus Fruitful

First, God despised the mountain. Then He thundered at it, "Before Zerubbabel you shall become a plain!" He declared that the intimidating mountain would be leveled into a plain. On mountains, almost nothing fruitful grows; on plains, sprawling orchards and spacious gardens can be cultivated. God said He would turn a bleak, barren mountain into a fruitful plain.

The Lord said that when the temple was completed, the people would install the capstone (the final stone that completed the structure) with shouts of praise and grace. By shouting, "Grace, grace to it!", the people would express their confidence that God's grace would rest on the temple and make it a blessing in the earth.

The mountain was the unfinished temple; the plain was the completed building project. Once the temple was finished, it would become a fruit-bearing plain that would strengthen God's people with spiritual nourishment. The life of God would flow through the sacrifices and worship of the temple and release divine favor on the nation of Israel so the people could succeed in life.

Golgotha Was a Desolate Mountain

When I think of a mountain being turned into a plain, the best example that comes to mind is Mount Golgotha. If ever there was a dark, bleak, desolate, lonely mountain, it was Golgotha. But Jesus labored hard on the cross and endured in faith, and look what the Father did with that mountain: He leveled it into a plain! Golgotha has become a fruitful plain that feeds the whole world.

Now, the cross of Christ is a template for *your* journey. Just as Jesus labored strenuously on the cross, you will also labor in your fiery trial. Go to work! Labor in the word and in the Spirit, and endure in faith—until you overcome. Never relent until your mountain becomes a plain that feeds your generation on God's goodness.

God Will Speak to Your Mountain

A "great mountain" is a foreboding monolith that represents darkness, loneliness, wilderness, beasts of prey, wild forests, looming impossibilities, sinister dread, and limited options. A plain represents the hopeful possibilities of many buildings, many people, businesses, institutions, agriculture, prosperity, and productivity.

The difference between a mountain and a plain is seen vividly in some of the cities that sit on the eastern edge of the Rocky Mountain Range. The city of Denver, for example, sits on a vast plain right next to the Rockies. It's home to millions of people, and it's a bustling city filled with houses, restaurants, stores, schools, industries, businesses, roads, malls, banks, universities, etc. Open plains, like the one on which Denver sits, present almost

You couldn't be resurrected until Jesus was. His cross justified you, but only His resurrection could raise you up.

limitless possibilities for development.

When you drive west from Denver into the Rocky Mountains, the change is immediate and stark. It's almost like you can draw a line on the ground where the plain stops and the mountain begins. Cross that line and you go, in one moment, from a bustling plain to a barren, lonely mountain. Suddenly, the banks stop; the restaurants stop; the industries stop; the schools stop. On a plain you can build almost anything, but very little is built on mountains. Developers tend to leave the rocky crags of mountain passes alone.

Here's the message of Zechariah's vision: God wants to turn your bleak, foreboding, impossible mountain into a fruitful plain where people are fed, great things are built, and new possibilities flourish.

When God spoke to Zerubbabel's mountain, He was also prophesying by implication to the impossible terrain of *your* fiery trial. Your circumstances loom before you like a dark mountain, but God has something to say to it: "You shall become a plain!" As you endure in faith in your crucifixion, God promises that a time will come when He, by His supernatural power, will level your mountain into a fruitful plain and resurrect you in a way that blesses your generation. When your mountain gets leveled into a plain, they'll build a city like Denver on it!

At the cross, God turned a mountain into a plain, and He has the same purpose for your trial. He intends to turn your horrible mountain of impossibilities into a plain of limitless potential. The God who leveled Golgotha is going to turn *your* mountain into a plain, too.

What can we learn from Zechariah's vision? *Endure!* Receive grace to do the hard labor in your fiery trial. As you endure in faith long-term, even in the midst of adversity, God will level your mountain into a plain that feeds a generation on God's goodness. May great and eternal things be built on the plain of your story!

For Group Study and Discussion

1. Take time this week to read Zechariah 4 carefully, go deep on the verses of your choice, and share your gleanings with the group.

2. Do you face a foreboding mountain that is a who? What's the name of your mountain? Tell us about the spiritual warfare you've faced.

3. God despised Zerubbabel's mountain because to Him it was nothing. Can you tell of a time when you realized God scorned the forces resisting you?

4. God turns mountains into fruitful plains. Can you think of a story that illustrates that truth—either from Scripture, or from history?

5. Golgotha was a mountain that God turned into a fruitful plain. Talk about it, and marvel at the wonder of the cross.

6. Zechariah prophesied to Zerubbabel's mountain, "You shall become a plain!" As you close in prayer, are there any mountains faced by anyone in your group to which you want to make that same declaration?

CHAPTER EIGHTEEN

The Warfare of the Cross Part 1

When you stand before Golgotha and behold the cross, something tells you that you're looking at a war zone. And you're right—Golgotha hosted the greatest battle of human history.

A Cosmic Conflict

When the Father spoke of Golgotha for the first time, He cast the crucifixion as a great, cosmic conflict. His first mention of it was in the garden of Eden, in a conversation with Satan. Addressing the serpent, He said, "He shall bruise your head, and you shall bruise His heel" (Gen 3:15). He meant that Jesus would bruise Satan's head, and that Satan would bruise Jesus' heel at the cross.

On that occasion, God was speaking from an eternal perspective about the cross; but during His crucifixion, Jesus' feelings were gripped by the immediacy of the agony. Hanging with nails in His hands and feet, that moment didn't feel to Jesus like a mere bruising of His heel; it felt like His entire being was being crushed, particle by particle—because it was.

The same is true for you. When you're in the vortex of your fiery trial, you feel like you're being pulled apart molecule by molecule—because you probably are. But when God planned this crucifixion for you, He saw it from a heavenly, bird's-eye perspective. And one day you're going to gain His eternal perspective on your trial. In that day, you'll see today's crushing trial for what it really is—a mere bruising of your heel.

Today, Jesus sees His crucifixion from a heavenly vantage. If we could have a personal conversation with Him right now about His cross, I think He might talk about it something like this: "Wow, that was intense, I really took it in the heel. But my adversary has been bloodied in the head!"

Jesus gave him a headache he'll never forget.

You may be in a trial that's killing you right now, but one day you're going to look back on today's crushing with a totally different perspective. Why? Because instead of giving up, you're praying, you're encouraging yourself in the promises of God, you're devoting yourself to loving Him, and you're holding tenaciously to His word. The time will come when you'll stand in the company of the overcomers and say something like, "Wow, that was intense. I really took it in the heel. But my adversary has been bloodied in the head!"

Yes, dearly beloved, I'm suggesting that God wants to use your trial to bloody the head of your adversary. By the time it's done, you will do more damage to your enemy than if the trial had never happened. Just as he deeply regrets taking on Jesus at the cross, may he also regret the day he took you on.

Calvary was a galactic boxing ring where Jesus and Satan went at it. Both were aiming for each other's head, but Satan only hit the heel. Jesus, on the other hand, made His mark. If you want to learn about spiritual warfare, therefore, don't go to the adversary. He's not that good. Instead, go to the Master. He's willing to take you on as His apprentice and teach you spiritual warfare.

Personally, I'm a big fan of Mel Gibson's movie, *The Passion of the Christ*. That movie helps me visualize just how bloody it was. He had blood on His scalp, blood on His head, blood on His face, blood on His neck, blood on His arms, blood on His hands, blood on His back, blood on His chest, blood on His legs, and blood on His feet. But make no mistake, Satan was more bloodied by the cross than Jesus Christ. Jesus was *wounded* by it, but Satan was *destroyed* by it.

One day you're going to look back on today's crushing and actually despise your sufferings. Why? Because when you compare your wounds with those of your

When Jesus died for you, He meant for you to take it personally.

enemy, you will have taken a blow to the heel, but he will have taken a blow to the head.

Are you the kind of Christian who wants to do damage to the kingdom of darkness? Then you may take something in the heel. Epic victories come at a price. There are some keys that, if You are to handle them, You must have scars in Your hands. If Jesus couldn't conquer Satan without incurring scars, what makes me think I can? If I have no scar, was I even in the battle? But He dignifies the scars we incur in this struggle and makes them trophies of grace.

Jesus, make me Your apprentice and teach me how to lay a blow to the head of my adversary.

We're in a War Zone

When God created man, He could have placed him on any inhabitable planet in any galaxy, but He chose to place him on the only planet in the entire universe that was inhabited by the devil. Why? Because from Day One of creation, God was picking a fight. He set the whole thing up to be a massive war zone between Adam's progeny and Satan's minions. Nothing of eternal value is ever accomplished on earth apart from warfare. We can't escape the law of warfare that governs all human affairs: Good advances only with a fight. The cross is the ultimate emblem of that reality, because God's kingdom could be established only through the warfare of the cross.

Spiritual warfare is intense, and our role in the battle is very real. God is the primary warrior in spiritual warfare, but we must fight, too. It's true that God commands victories for His people (Ps 44:4), but you're going to have to go out there and fight for them. For example, God brought the temple down on the Philistines with a great slaughter, but Samson had to find the pillars of the temple and push with all his might. Therefore, get ready for war. Your only way forward is through intense spiritual struggle.

Our engagement in spiritual warfare is directly connected to our identity as kings to God. In ancient times, the primary function of a king was to lead his nation in warfare (1 Sam 8:20; 10:1). Kings went to war, it's just what they did. They were considered successful when they could lead their army in conquest and infuse the nation's economy with the spoils of war.

The Bible says we've been made kings and priests to God (1 Pet 2:9; Rev 1:6; 3:21; 20:6). As priests, we minister to the Lord in His courts; as kings, we do spiritual exploits to advance His interests in the earth. As kings to God, we have the privilege, in the words of Reinhard Bonnke, to plunder hell and populate heaven. Our function as kings is *militant*.

Jesus came as a King—the King of the Jews. As such, He came for conquest. At the cross, the King of kings declared war on sin, Satan, death, and hell. His resurrection proved that He overcame. And now He invites us, as kings, to become players with Him in our planet's titanic clash between good and evil. We're always seeking, therefore, to become more skilled in spiritual warfare.

King Jesus is the Master Warrior, and I'm His apprentice. In the lingo of *Star Wars*, He's my Jedi Knight, and I'm His padawan learner. He's training me to become more like Him—effective in spiritual warfare.

When the King wants to instruct you in spiritual warfare, He uses Mount Calvary as your training ground. This is where He won the greatest battle ever fought, and this is where He'll teach you how to fight. When I look at the cross, I realize that this is how I fight my battles.

The cross is our template for spiritual warfare.

A title was written above His bloody, thorn-crowned brow: "Jesus of Nazareth, the King of the Jews" (John 19:19). When you come to the cross, you're looking at our King, the Commander-In-Chief, as He leads to war.

> David bested Goliath with a stick and five stones; Jesus bested Satan with a stick and five wounds.

The disciples thought He had come to conquer Rome, but He was after a much bigger target. Had He come down from the cross, He could have conquered Rome; but He stayed on the cross so He could conquer death, hell, the grave, and Satan. He died a spotless Lamb, descended to hell, overcame hell, plundered it, resurrected with the plunder in hand, and with it gave gifts to men (Eph 4:8).[1] He's a mighty Warrior-King!

Three Thieves

When the devil tempted Jesus for forty days in the wilderness, he offered to *give* Jesus the kingdoms of this world (all Jesus had to do was worship him). But instead, Jesus decided He was going to *take* the kingdoms of this world from the devil. Jesus was like, "You're not going to give them to Me, I'm going to steal them from you."

I always thought there were two thieves crucified on Calvary, but now I realize that, in a certain sense, there were three. The Man on the middle cross was also a Thief. Can you see God's poetry in framing His Thief between two others?

You might be wondering, *What did Jesus steal?*

Well, for starters, He stole the show. All eyes were riveted on the middle cross.

He stole from Satan the rulership over the kingdoms of this world.

He stole our souls from the clutches of Death.

He stole those held captive in Hades and led them forth in triumphant procession.

He stole the keys of Hades and Death from the devil.

And He stole my heart. I'll love Him forever!

What's more, for those who long for His appearing, He's returning as a Thief so He can spring us from this mess.

---

1   By the way, David did the same thing. He conquered the Amalekites and then distributed the plunder as gifts to the elders of Judah (1 Sam 30:26). He was showing he had the moxie of a king.

Yes, I think *three* thieves were crucified that day.

Satan Was Cast Out

In speaking of His impending crucifixion, Jesus said, "Now the ruler of this world will be cast out" (John 12:31). Jesus acknowledged that Satan was who he claimed to be— the ruler of this world (Luke 4:6). But at the cross, he would be cast out.

Now, the question is, *From where was Satan cast out?* The answer comes clearer when we identify that there are five times in Scripture when Satan is *cast out*. The first time he was cast out was when he and his angels were cast from heaven to earth at his fall (Luke 10:18). The second time he was cast out was at the cross, according to John 12:31 which is quoted above. The next three castings are future events. The third time he will be cast out will be in a war with Michael and his angels (Rev 12:7-9). Right now Satan has a place of advantage in heavenly places over the earth, but the day is coming when he'll be cast down to earth and will be more limited and confined in his activities. The fourth time he'll be cast into the bottomless pit (Rev 20:3). And at the fifth casting, he'll be cast into the lake of fire (Rev 20:10).

Five times he said in his heart, "I will," as he sought to lift his throne up, up, up, and be like the Most High (Isa 14:13-14). Therefore, he will be cast down five times, with each casting being successively down, down, down.

Once again, the second casting out happened at the cross, as Jesus said. "Now the ruler of this world will be cast out" (John 12:31). And again, our question is, *From where was Satan cast out at the cross?* The answer is to be found right in John 12:31. At the cross, Satan was cast out from his position and office as *the ruler of this world.* His authority was downgraded. He's still "the god of this age" (2 Cor 4:4) because

He prayed like a Lion and died like a Lamb.

he's obeyed and worshiped by the people of this age, and he's still "the prince of the power of the air" (Eph 2:2), a position of advantage he will hold in heavenly places until the third casting out (Rev 12:7-9). But he's no longer the ruler of this world—Jesus is. When He rose, He told His disciples, "All authority has been given to Me in heaven and on earth" (Matt 28:18). He's now "the ruler over the kings of the earth" (Rev 1:5). Jesus is the Ruler of the kingdoms of this world—a position He stole from Satan at the cross.

It bears repeating: The cross was the most dramatic military excursion of human history because Satan was cast out as ruler of this world, sin and death and Hades were defeated, and hell was plundered of the souls of the saints who were waiting for their deliverance from death (Eph 4:8).

I'm going somewhere with this. Please come to the next chapter as we continue to speak of the warfare of the cross, because I want you to see how this applies to the way you engage in spiritual warfare.

For Group Study and Discussion

1. Talk about the cross as a battle. What forces do you see engaging in this battle?

2. Are you in a spiritual fight right now? In what way does your trial feel like much more than just a mere bruising of your heel? Is God preparing you to lay a blow to the head of your adversary?

3. Find the statement, *If Jesus couldn't conquer Satan without incurring scars, what makes me think I can?* Talk about the content of that paragraph, and what it means to you.

4. The author suggests we can see Jesus as a Thief on the cross. Does this picture warm your heart to the beauty of Jesus?

5. Study the five times Satan is cast out, and be ready to talk about this when the group gathers. Is there anything about this that helps you in your walk?

6. As you close, look at the cross as your template for spiritual warfare, and let Genesis 3:15 guide your prayers.

CHAPTER NINETEEN
The Warfare of the Cross Part 2

Spiritual warfare is often exercised through prayer. We shouldn't be too surprised, therefore, when Satan attacks our prayer lives. He'll do anything in his power to stop us from praying. The place of prayer is the place of warfare. We see this in the lives of Samuel, Daniel, and Jesus—each of them was attacked precisely when they went to pray.

How Samuel Was Attacked

In the days of the judges and Eli the priest, the nation of Israel was not doing well spiritually. They were oppressed by the Philistines, and the Philistines had even managed to capture the ark of the covenant in one of the wars. Eventually the ark was returned, but it was being stored at a temporary residence. Now, under Samuel's leadership, the nation lamented after the Lord and wanted to return to Him in repentance.

To facilitate their repentance, Samuel called a national prayer meeting (1 Sam 7:3-6). The people put away their idols and gathered together to seek the Lord.

When the Philistines saw that all Israel had assembled in one location, they viewed it as the perfect opportunity to attack. They found it difficult to ferret out the Israelites when they were dispersed across the countryside, but once they were gathered together, the Philistines considered them an easy target.

Here's the point: When Israel gathered to pray, the enemy attacked.

How Daniel Was Attacked

Daniel's enemies were out to get him, and the only way they knew to undermine

What kind of Man, instead of trembling in trepidation, is prophesying as He climbs the hill to His crucifixion? (Luke 23:29).

him was to accuse him regarding His devotion to God. They got the king to pass a law that made it illegal to pray to any god but the king for the next thirty days. When Daniel heard that legislation had been passed, he went straight home and, according to his daily custom, opened the window of his house toward Jerusalem and prayed to His God.

His enemies were waiting and watching. When they saw him kneel toward Jerusalem and pray, they pounced. Daniel ended up spending that night in the lion's den.

Again, the point is this: When Daniel prayed, his enemies attacked.

How Jesus Was Attacked

Jesus often prayed in Gethsemane with His disciples and, as one of the twelve, Judas Iscariot knew the spot well. On the night of Jesus' arrest, Judas led a group of soldiers and armed leaders to the garden, and sure enough, Jesus was there in prayer.

Jesus was arrested by His enemies in the place of prayer.

I'm reiterating this point: The place of prayer is the place of spiritual warfare. When you're a person of prayer, you won't have to go looking for a fight; it will come to you. Satan attacks you *because* you're a person of prayer.

You do your best fighting when you're on your knees.

When we examine Jesus' prayer life, we're able to see exactly how He entered into warfare on the cross.

What Was the Nature of the Warfare?

When we look at the cross, we realize a cosmic struggle was taking place, but it's not readily evident exactly what the nature of the battle was. It seems certain that Jesus and Satan were fighting, but in what manner? How was Satan attacking Him, and how was Jesus fighting back? We're going to find the answer in Jesus' prayer life.

In Gethsemane—Jesus' place of prayer—He revealed to His disciples the nature of the warfare when He said, "Watch and pray, lest you enter into temptation" (Mark 14:38). He was alerting them that the warfare regarded *temptation*. In the events that were about to transpire, they would be tempted to sin. For example, they would be tempted to fight in fleshly ways, and they would be tempted to abandon Him in terror and flee. Jesus urged them to pray with eyes wide open. If they would pray, they would be able to resist and overcome temptation; if they would disengage and nod off, they would likely enter into temptation.

Notice that Jesus urged them to *watch*. This means we should be watchful regarding current events and things happening around us. We should be attentive to distinguish the respective activities of God, Satan, and people. Then He told them to *pray*. In other words, after observing everything around us, we should talk things over with God, not people. If we watch and then talk to people, we won't find the strength and discernment we need to resist temptation. To engage effectively in spiritual warfare, we must watch and pray.

Jesus didn't hold a huddle in Gethsemane with His disciples and say, "Judas is about to betray Me. He's on his way here with a group of armed soldiers to arrest Me. Got any input on how we should handle this?" He didn't say watch and *chat*, but watch and *pray*.

In Gethsemane, He prayed like a Lion so He could die like a Lamb. He had to win it in prayer before He could win it on the cross.

He prayed in Gethsemane so He wouldn't enter into temptation on the cross. He gathered His reserves in prayer so He could endure the cross without entering into temptation.

Through prayer, we access the strength we need from the Spirit to face and overcome the enemy. Prayer is our supply line

> Don't serve a god who can't save himself. Serve the One who saved Himself from Hades and Death.

in our war with temptation. It's essential to identify your supply lines so you can protect them.

When you enlist in the armed forces, one of the first military laws they'll teach you is, *Protect your supply lines.* They'll remind you that Hitler lost World War II largely because his tanks ran out of fuel and his troops ran out of food. Hitler repeated a deadly tactical error: He pushed his troops to fronts his supply chain couldn't maintain. Before going into spiritual warfare, therefore, get your supply lines functional.

In Gethsemane, Jesus was getting fueled up in the Spirit so He could expend Himself on the cross. When He strode toward Calvary, He walked like a Man ready for battle. He wasn't trembling in fear as He climbed the hill, He was prophesying (Luke 23:29). What kind of Warrior prophesies as He marches toward His crucifixion? A great King who is fueled up, mighty to save, and ready to engage the enemy.

The warfare of the cross was simply this: Satan was tempting Jesus to sin on the cross, and Jesus was resisting so that He wouldn't enter temptation.

The nature of our warfare in the battle is precisely the same. He tries to get us to enter into temptation, and we resist him. In other words, he tries to incite us to sin, and we fight to endure in faith without sinning.

This is how we fight our battles.

Applied to Our Current War

At the time of this writing (2020), America feels like a war zone. We're in a war against coronavirus (COVID-19), racial tensions are at a boiling point across our nation, and we're in a political war between Democrats and Republicans. The atmosphere is so charged that some have wondered if America might be on the precipice of a civil war.

What is Satan's agenda for Americans in this current milieu? He wants from us what he wanted from Jesus on the cross: *He wants us to sin.* He wants Person A to sin against Person B, and then for Person B to sin back against Person A; and then for Person C to sin against both Person A and Person B; and then for Person D to sin against Person C; and then for Person E to sin against A, B, C, and D; and then for Persons A, B, C, and D to sin against Persons E, F, G, and H. In other words, Satan wants everyone sinning against everyone else, all the time.

According to my friend, Daniel Lim, Satan is enraged at human privilege. Humans are getting from God everything that he wanted. He tried to *steal* it from God and was denied; and now, God is just *giving* it to us! Jesus stole what Satan tried to give Him (the kingdoms of this world), so He could give us what Satan tried to steal (the Father's fortune). People of every skin color, every race, every language, and every nation are inheriting the family fortune together with Jesus. We're being given everything Satan wanted, and he's so enraged by our human privilege that he devotes himself tirelessly to tempting us to sin against each another.

Satan loves it when we enter into anger, rage, hatred, bitterness, injustice, accusation, blame, contentions, dissensions, impatience, malice, unforgiveness, and murder. He wants us declaring war on one another.

First John 3:8 says, "He who sins is of the devil, for the devil has sinned from the beginning. For this purpose the Son of God was manifested, that He might destroy the works of the devil." *What are the works of the devil?* The verse tells us. *The devil sins*—that's what his works are. He's always been sinning, and He's always wanting us to share in his sins. Jesus, however, came to destroy the power of sin over our lives. He went to the cross to liberate us from its tyranny.

Our biggest enemy is actually not the devil. Our biggest enemy is sin. Why? Because sins kills us. The devil probably

> If the cross demonstrates the intensity of the Father's training of His sons, the resurrection is the exoneration of His kindness toward them.

can't kill you, but sin certainly can. Sin imprisons people here in this life, and then it imprisons them forever in hell.

The flashpoint in spiritual warfare is sin.

Satan Tempted Jesus to Sin

During the crucifixion, Satan did everything in his power to tempt Jesus to sin. He hoped that Jesus would be weakened enough, through the intensity of His sufferings, to enter into temptation.

If Satan could have successfully provoked Jesus to sin on the cross, the consequences would have been catastrophic:

- Jesus would not have died a spotless Lamb.
- He would have died for His own sin.
- Our salvation would have been forfeited.
- Death and Hades would have been able to hold Him.
- There would have been no resurrection.
- All would have been lost for the human race.

But on the other hand, if Jesus will be able to endure His sufferings and die without entering into temptation, the implications will be monumental:

- He will die a sinless, spotless Lamb.
- He will purchase redemption for the entire human race.
- He will descend to hell in Holiness, preach to the souls in prison, and instigate a rumble heard round the universe.
- Sin, death, Hades, and Satan will be defeated.
- He will resurrect from Hades and take captivity captive with Him in His festal train (Eph 4:8).

Hades was not prepared to host Holiness. Hell's plan was for Jesus to sin on the cross, but instead, He died in Holiness.

When Holiness showed up, hell didn't know what to do with Him. Every demon in hell knew the story was going to end badly for them. On the third day, Holiness resurrected from the dead (Rom 1:4).

During His days on the earth, Jesus overcame sin, the world, and the flesh. Then, in His death, He overcame sickness, sorrows, the curse of the law, and all of Satan's forces. At His resurrection, He overcame death, hell and the grave. What a heroic, magnificent Champion! And what a wonderful gospel He's given us!

You may recall that, when David defeated the Amalekites, he gathered and distributed the plunder to his friends in Judah. Well, when the Son of David resurrected from hell, He followed suit. Our Warrior-King plundered Satan and hell, brought the plunder up with Him, and distributed gifts freely to all His saints (Eph 4:8).

And again, all of this was because *He did not enter into temptation on the cross.*

Now we're going to look at the two primary ways Satan tempted Jesus on the cross. We need the next chapter to complete our exploration of *the warfare of the cross.*

> Live in the shadow of the cross and let it drive all frivolity and foolish banter from your soul.

For Group Study and Discussion

1. *Satan attacks us in the place of prayer*: How have you experienced this? Talk about the statement, *You do your best fighting when you're on your knees.*

2. Our warfare regards *temptation*. Go after this idea—can you find it in other Scriptures? Bring your insights to the group discussion.

3. Satan wanted Jesus to enter into temptation and sin during the crucifixion. What did Jesus do to stay strong?

4. Talk about our culture wars today, and how Satan wants us to sin against each other. How does the cross address our culture wars?

5. How do you think Satan tempted Jesus to compromise His love, and lose faith during His agony?

6. As you close, offer prayers based on Mark 14:38.

CHAPTER TWENTY

The Warfare of the Cross Part 3

We said in the last chapter that Satan was present at the crucifixion, tempting Jesus to sin. But now let's be more specific. *How* was he tempting Him? First of all, he tried to provoke Jesus to become angry and defensive. So much animosity was coming against Him, and Satan wanted Him, in the midst of His suffering, to become angry at the injustice of it all. He used every device in his arsenal to incite Jesus to become angry, resentful, bitter, or offended.

Satan Tempted Jesus to Become Angry

One way Satan did this was by making His enemies rabid with hatred. He stirred the envy of the Jews and caused them to attack Jesus with malicious cruelty. Their rage was so irrational that they actually called for the release of a murderer named Barabbas so that Jesus would be condemned. Satan hoped their animosity would trigger a sinful response in Jesus. Instead, He loved them even while they assailed Him.

Then Satan stirred the animosity of the Roman soldiers. When the Jewish leaders turned Jesus over to Pilate for sentencing, the soldiers vented their frustration and anti-Semitism on Jesus. They scourged Him, beat Him, crowned Him with thorns, drove the thorns into His head, and abused Him in whatever manner they desired. Again, Satan wanted Jesus to become angry and resentful at the unjust treatment. But instead of hating them, He forgave them. His love for them was so strong that they were incapable of overwhelming it. He was like, *There's nothing you can do to Me to make Me hate you, or threaten you, or revile you, or strike back at you.* He loved them to the end.

Well, if Jesus won't get angry at His persecutors, can He be induced to become

Satan, confront the Lamb on the cross and you'll face the Lion in Hades.

angry at His Father? After all, the Father was emptying the cup of His wrath on Jesus, and He didn't deserve it.

During the crucifixion, Satan kept yammering at Jesus with an incessant deluge of lies. We know he was always looking for an occasion to tempt Him (Luke 4:13), and the cross seemed to be the ultimate opportunity. So he came after Jesus with a vengeance, hitting Him with every conceivable temptation. We're not told what kinds of lies he battered Jesus with, but they may have sounded like, "Your Father has rejected You. He has set you up for failure. He got Your hopes up with huge promises, but now that You need Him most, He's abandoned You. He's an oppressive, abusive tyrant. Can't You see this? It's so wrong what He's doing to You! What kind of a Father do you have, anyway? Is this the way a good Father loves His Son? Admit it, He's completely dysfunctional. He's left You here an orphan. I'm giving You one last chance to curse Your Father, and I'll get You off this cross and give You Your life back. Curse Him!"

How Jesus responded to the temptations is not shown in the Gospels, but it's revealed by David in Psalm 22—a Messianic psalm about the cross. Here's what David had Jesus saying on the cross:

> My God, My God, why have You forsaken Me? …But You are holy (Psalm 22:1, 3).

Instead of echoing Satan's accusations, Jesus said to His Father, "You are holy." To explain the significance of that statement, I want to show what's behind the word *holy*.

Jesus Worshiped His Father

When you say to God, "You are holy," you're honoring His majesty. There are basically two ways you can express your worship. On the one hand, you can say things like, "You are kind, You are tender, You're compassionate and merciful, gracious, dependable, unchanging, unrivaled, unique, beau-tiful, righteous, just, strong, mighty, omnipotent, omniscient, omnipresent, wise, discerning, healing, delivering, saving, helping, redeeming, restoring, carrying, caring, humble, longsuffering, good, true, bright, fiery, jealous, wrathful, judging, vengeful, enlightening, unstoppable, transcendent, immanent, patient, faithful, brilliant, excellent, enduring, unpredictable, living, enlivening, pure, undefiled, blameless, able, equitable, glorious, majestic, eternal, immortal, invisi-ble, burning, jealous, loving, enthroned, militant, victorious, conquering, forgiving, cleansing, immovable, unshakable, wonderful, unsearchable, and unfathomable."

Or, on the other hand, to say all of that at once, you can say, "You are holy." *Holy* is all His wonderful attributes bound up in one glorious word.

When Jesus said to His Father, "You are holy," He was saying, "You're perfect, wise, kind, and compassionate. I love You!" He was worshiping and loving His Father while hanging on the nails—a side of the cross shown to us only by David.

Jesus had no accusation toward His Father, even though His Father was killing Him. But it wasn't just an absence of ac-cusation that characterized Christ's attitude; He actually *dig-nified* His Father's crushing. "You've forsaken Me, but You're perfect in all Your ways. The way You're handling Me right now is right, wise, and good. You are holy!"

Satan wanted Jesus' love for His Father to collapse while suffering at Calvary, but Jesus was ready for this temptation. He just kept praying. With everything coming at Him, He just kept loving the people driving the nails in His hands and lov-ing His heavenly Father. He passed the love test.

Satan Tempted Jesus to Become Discouraged

The first prong of Satan's attack was against Jesus' love, to make Him bitter. The second prong of his attack was against

> The cross is your doing nothing and His doing everything.

His faith. If Satan couldn't make Jesus resentful on the cross, perhaps he could discourage Him and cause Him to lose heart. The reason this was important is because, "Whatever is not of faith is sin" (Rom 14:23). If Jesus were to sin by losing faith during His sufferings, then He would not die a blameless Lamb, and Hades would be able to hold Him.

On the cross, Jesus fought "the good fight of faith" (1 Tim 6:12). Everything about crucifixion was designed to overwhelm its victims with discouragement, despair, and hopelessness. To stay in faith, Jesus had to *fight*. He had to use the shield of faith because Satan was assaulting Him with all his fiery darts (Eph 6:16).

We're not told what lies Satan used in that moment, but they were probably along the lines of, "You'll never recover from this. Never again will You see Your Father's face. You're going to descend to hell and never get out. I've got You exactly where I want You. I'm going to torment You forever. The Father's plan has failed. Your wound is incurable, and nobody can save You from death. You're mine now."

Discouragement tried to conquer Christ's heart and gut His soul, but Isaiah spoke of this moment when he prophesied, "He will not fail nor be discouraged, till He has established justice in the earth" (Isa 42:4). Jesus never lost faith in His Father's power and good purposes.

Jesus remained strong in faith because of His knowledge. Isaiah testified, "By His knowledge My righteous Servant shall justify many, for He shall bear their iniquities" (Isa 53:11). What did Jesus know? He knew His Father's eternal plans and purposes for redeeming humanity to Himself. On the cross, He remained confident in His Father's plan and power to pull it off.

Did you think Jesus was naked on the cross? No. He was wearing the belt of truth, the breastplate of righteousness, the helmet of salvation, the shield of faith, and the sword of the Spirit (Eph 6:14-17). He got dressed in prayer so that He wouldn't enter into temptation.

I wonder what He said to His Father while draining the cup. Perhaps it sounded something like, "Abba, You are holy. You are good. Your plan is perfect, and You're going to finish what You've started. You're going to win them from every nation and language, You're going to save, redeem, heal. and deliver them. You're going to call them, justify them, glorify them, crown them, and seat them with Me on My throne. You're going to raise Me up, and then You're going to raise them up. I know Your power, and I know You're going to complete this work. You are holy!"

Jesus never sinned by losing faith. He drank the cup to the bottom, cried out, "It is finished," and died the spotless Lamb of God.

How strong do You have to be to drink the Father's cup, endure the assaults of Satan, and suffer the agonies of crucifixion without sinning? *Real* strong! Oh, He's strong, dearly beloved! He's a mighty Warrior who is strong to deliver and mighty to save! You can trust Him with your heart.

Satan Attacks Us in the Same Way

Our warfare is exactly the same as Christ's on the cross. The enemy attacks our faith and love because he wants *us* to sin. If you want to learn how to resist him, look to Jesus' example. This is how we fight our battles. Again, the cross is our template for spiritual warfare.

The devil came after Jesus like a roaring lion, and he comes after us in the same way, seeking whom he may devour (1 Pet 5:8). How does he devour us? By tempting us to sin. Demons are like hungry lions, salivating to devour us with temptation (Isa 35:9).

Lions roar to communicate with other lions and to announce ownership of their pride. But even more significantly, lions

Jesus, don't You have resurrection as Your goal? But no, He's got His eyes on the scroll (Rev 5:7).

roar to terrorize their prey. When disoriented, prey will over-react and be more susceptible to capture. Thus, Satan roars to intimidate us with every temptation possible.

When you're in a fiery trial, the enemy tries to take advantage of your weakened state by tempting you. Someone might look at my fiery trial and wonder, *Bob, have you sinned in your trial?* Yes, I have. But that doesn't mean I'm disqualified. Jesus is my Jedi Knight, and I'm His padawan learner, His apprentice. He's teaching me spiritual warfare in the journey. Only Jesus got it perfect; we learn as we stumble our way forward and keep our eyes on Him.

How does Satan tempt us in our trials? He'll try to make our love grow cold and our faith fail. He tries to deceive, to distract us from prayer, and to discourage our souls. He wants us to shrink back from God. He'll try to make us bitter or angry. He wants us to accuse and blame others, to demand our rights, and to fight for our lives. In other words, he wants us to sin.

But God has a different plan for your life. He wants you to walk the course of everyday life without caving to sin. His grace will give you the strength to always prefer others, always show honor and kindness to your enemies, consider others better than yourself, never strike back, and season every word of your mouth with salt. He wants you always laying your life down, always losing your life, always hating your life, always giving, and always being hospitable. His purpose is that you be patient, believing the best in others, forgiving those who wrong you, and joyfully accepting the plundering of your goods (Heb 10:34). He will help you to praise Him at all times, worship Him, fear Him, talk to Him about everything, remain confident in His goodness, and rejoice in His goodness.

We pray so that, instead of entering into temptation, we can live like this every day of our lives.

Do you understand the power of living in holiness? That power is never seen more clearly than at the cross. Jesus died in pure holiness (without entering into temptation) and descended to Hades. Holiness proved to be stronger than death, hell, Satan, and the grave. On the third day, He resurrected and then ascended to heaven where He sat down with His Father on His throne (Rev 3:21). Holiness resurrected from the dead (Rom 1:4), and nothing has changed; Holiness *still* resurrects and ascends to the highest places. God's agenda for your journey is *holiness*.

No matter how dark your pit, how strong your challenge, or how ominous your mountain—live in holiness! Holiness rises again. Listen as He speaks this word to your heart: "To him who overcomes I will grant to sit with Me on My throne, as I also overcame and sat down with My Father on His throne" (Rev 3:21).

Watch and pray! This is how we fight our battles. Jesus has freed us from the tyranny of sin, and now we're able to overcome temptation.

As you hold this book in your hand, what kind of warfare are you facing? Is it in your marriage or family? Is it in your career or at your workplace? Is it among friends or neighbors or enemies? Watch and pray, and the Holy Spirit will empower you to overcome. When you walk the course of everyday life in holiness, you bring life and grace to every person you touch. You're the salt of the earth and the light of the world.

Why Did Satan Crucify Jesus?

Satan helped instigate the crucifixion of Christ. How? Well, he fueled the insane envy of the Jewish leaders so they would deliver Jesus to Pilate (Mark 15:10), and he commandeered Judas Iscariot to betray Jesus to the arresting officers (John 13:27). Clearly, Satan schemed to kill Jesus.

But why? After all, Jesus had repeatedly prophesied His arrest and death, and it would appear that Satan played into Jesus'

> The angel rolled back the tombstone, sat on it, and basically went, "I broke your Roman seal. Got anything to say about that?"

hand. Why would Satan actively pursue Christ's death even after He had predicted it? Because he's a *gambler*.

We know from the story of Job that Satan is a compulsive gambler. He's always working the odds. The cross was a huge gamble for him, but it seemed his best bet to get to Jesus, find a chink in His armor, and provoke Him to sin. An excruciating death was like the ace in Satan's hand.

Satan was gambling on two things. First, he was gambling that Jesus, in the throes of consummate suffering, would become so weak that He could be induced to sin. And if that didn't work, he had a second bet on which he was wagering.

Satan was wagering that Death could overpower Jesus. Remember, he had lived in the courts of heaven and knew something about God's power. But now, with his home in Hades, he was witnessing the power of Death. Death was stronger than everything and everyone that had come under its power. It was an uncreated power that knew no rival. It was far stronger than Satan himself, and he knew it. Satan knew he was no match for Jesus, but he was willing to gamble that Death was. He may have thought, "I don't think God realizes just how powerful Death really is. I think He underestimates it. If I can get Jesus under the power of Death, I bet He'll be unable to escape." If sin couldn't take Jesus out, Satan was willing to bet that Death could.

Satan's gamble was huge. If hell and Death could hold Jesus, Satan's reign would continue. But if Jesus could overcome Death and resurrect from hell, Satan would lose everything.

To overthrow Satan, Jesus had to accomplish two great feats. First, He had to overcome temptation by not sinning on the cross. Then, after descending to hell, He had to overcome Death. Hades had to be opened from the inside.[1]

Just as with Job, once again Satan lost the bet. Jesus overcame both sin and Hades. On the third day, our Champion

---

1   See my book on this topic, entitled, *Opened From the Inside.*

bested the powers of hell and rose from the dead. Inside that Man was a power that a confederation of Death, hell, Satan, and the grave couldn't conquer.

Resurrection! Let's go there. In the last three chapters, we've explored the warfare of the cross. Now let's look at that which Jesus fought to attain: Resurrection!

> When the Man you've been following around the country dies and then resurrects to life, it puts grit in your spirit.

For Group Study and Discussion

1. Satan tempted Jesus on the cross to become angry, defensive, or offended. How have you been tempted to be offended in your warfare?

2. According to Psalm 22:3, Jesus worshiped on the cross. Talk about worship, and its role in helping us to endure without sinning.

3. *Worship dignifies the Father's crushing in our lives.* Unpack that statement. How can we dignify His ways when we're drinking a bitter cup?

4. "Whatever is not of faith is sin" (Rom 14:23). How has Satan tempted you to lose faith in the midst of your warfare?

5. What kind of knowledge do we need to pursue in the midst of trials? Search for answers in Scripture and bring your Scriptures to the discussion. How do we pursue this knowledge?

6. The author gives his perspective on why Satan crucified Jesus. What's your insight on that question?

7. As you close, use Psalm 22:3 to inspire your prayers.

CHAPTER TWENTY-ONE

Resurrection Is Essential

The cross and resurrection are inseparable. Any examination of the cross that doesn't include resurrection doesn't even see the cross. Why? Because the cross is not a stand-alone event. There's much more to the story than just crucifixion and death. The passion of Christ is an epic drama that spans several chapters: the betrayal, arrest, trial, scourging, crucifixion, death, descent to hell, resurrection, and ascension to heaven. The whole story is one seamless swing at sin, sickness, and death.

The cross ends with a semicolon; the period comes only after the resurrection and ascension. The cross can be understood only against the backdrop of resurrection, just as resurrection can be understood only against the backdrop of crucifixion. Resurrection confirmed both the validity and efficacy of the cross. The cross *without* resurrection is a miserable story to bury in the sands of time; the cross *with* resurrection is a nail-biting thriller that provides hope and redemption for the entire human race.

Let's look at the symbiotic relationship between crucifixion and resurrection, and then how we share in both.

As said earlier, the cross *without* resurrection is cosmic Child abuse; the cross *with* resurrection is glorious vindication and magnificent exaltation. Cynics looked at the cross and called it abusive, so it was critical to the Father's reputation that Jesus resurrect. Resurrection proved the Father's goodness, generosity, and wisdom. Resurrection, therefore, was not a nice add-on or luxury attachment; it was fundamentally essential to redemption's story. Cross and resurrection *must* go together.

Why is this important to us? In our personal journey of identification with Christ, God has destined for us to share in both His crucifixion and resurrection. His crucifixion helps us endure and make sense of our sufferings, and His resurrection gives us the confidence that we also will rise again. Paul articulated this hope in Romans 6:5, "For if we have been united together in the likeness of His death, certainly we also shall be in the likeness of His resurrection."

I'm going to say it again: The cross is never meant to be the last chapter of your story. From the beginning of your fiery trial, the Father always intended for your story to culminate in resurrection. Without resurrection, the story is simply incomplete. Crucifixion supplies a great plot and resurrection supplies a great finish.

Whenever there's a cross, there must also be a resurrection. That's always the Father's way. The cross provides a way for resurrection power to be unleashed in the earth. No cross, no resurrection. Great cross, great resurrection.

Crucifixion Is the Compelling Chapter

To grasp the symbiotic relationship between cross and resurrection, we must see that crucifixion is the power element in our story. Let me explain.

The power element in a story is the gripping part that people remember and talk about afterward. They rarely talk about the beautiful way the story resolved in the end, but rather the suspenseful moments in the saga when circumstances seemed impossible to overcome. Jesus' resurrection was glorious, but the power element of His passion was the cross (1 Cor 1:18). In the same way, when you're in the most agonizing part of your trial, you're actually in the power phase of your journey.

Your cross is your power alley—the part of your story that will compel the generations that follow. Cooperate with God, therefore, to build this part of your history with Him and make the story strong. After you've been raised up, it's not your

One word will resurrect you.

exaltation they'll be talking about, but your crucifixion. The suspense, drama, intrigue, mystery, nail-biting thrills—it all revolves around the intensity of your adversity. Resurrection brings resolve and honor, but crucifixion provides the compelling part of the story.

Again, God paints the agony of your journey against the backdrop of your resurrection. The contrast makes your crucifixion pop and rivets the next generation.

I'll use some Bible examples to illustrate my meaning.

Job. When someone mentions his name, your first thought isn't about how he was ultimately healed, regained double his wealth, saw God in a glory encounter, lived to a ripe, old age, and left behind a fruitful legacy. No, your first thought is, *The guy with boils. The guy whose friends turned on him. The guy who lost his children, his wealth, the support of his wife, and his emotional equilibrium.* When you think Job, you think horrific pain. We always remember best the most potent parts of a story. That's why we remember his boils and suffering. *His pain was the power part of the story.* When he was in the throes of his darkest hour, he probably didn't realize it at the time but he was actually in his power alley.

Joseph. When you think of Joseph, your first memory isn't that he became the number two man on the planet and saved the lives of everyone in Egypt. No, when you think Joseph you think prison. You think about his brothers' rejection, his stint in slavery, and his being innocently imprisoned for ten years. We're not encouraged primarily by his promotion to the palace, but by the admirable way he endured his bitter adversities.

While in prison, he agonized to understand God's purpose. He had no idea he was living a drama we'd be talking about ever since. His prison was his power alley because now it speaks to all the prisoners of every generation.

Hannah. When Hannah's name is mentioned, our first association isn't that she was the woman who mothered the prophet who would anoint the first king of Israel. Instead, our first thought is about the bitterness of her barrenness. When she wept in grief and reproach over her barrenness, she had no idea she was living the part of the story that would be remembered by people in the twenty-first century. We connect with her wailing heart because we, too, grapple with our own barrenness.

This principle is also true for you. When you're in your crucible of adversity, you're actually in the power part of your story. You're the building the part of your story they'll talk about for decades. Work with it, then. Maximize it. Make this part of your story strong. Give God material to work with. Paint the biggest bullseye on your chest you possibly can, and give Him room to craft a story for the generations.

Resurrection Validates Crucifixion

Crucifixion was Christ's compelling chapter, and then resurrection released its power to us. That's still how it works for us today. In our crucifixion we're in our power alley, and in our resurrection the story is released to others in a lifegiving way.

When you're being crucified, the jury's out on your finish. People will look at the spectacle of your life and wonder where it's going to go (Heb 10:33). They may think you've been forsaken by God. They may say, "God doesn't do this kind of thing." After all, that's what all of us first thought at the cross. We looked at His contorted figure and said, "This Man is suffering some kind of punishment because God doesn't do this kind of thing with His friends." Then, when God resurrected Him, we went, "Oops." The resurrection validated that God had orchestrated the crucifixion.

When God raises you up, "Many will see it and fear" (Ps 40:3) because it will mean He was the designer of your horrible pit. That will be fearful to observers because they will

> He died like a Lamb and rose like a Lion.

rightly conclude: *If God designed that prison for you, there's the possibility He might fashion one for me, too.* Your resurrection will cause others to tremble before the sovereignty of a jealous God. Said another way, your resurrection will show that God has been writing your story from start to finish—including all the adversity and agony.

Christ Arose!

This is the banner of our Gospel and it's the best news ever! Jesus purchased our salvation, rose from the grave, and then ascended to heaven where He serves as our Advocate to God. We serve a Savior who both died and rose again. The story is altogether stunning!

If someone were to suggest that Jesus *didn't* resurrect from the dead, then the story is absurd and leaves us with three questions that can't be answered:

1. If Jesus *didn't* resurrect from the grave, why didn't His death kill the movement?

Everybody knows: *Kill the leader, you kill the movement.* This is why the chief priests lobbied so fiercely for Jesus to be crucified. They wanted all His followers to look at His agony and get the message: *Continue to follow this Man and you'll share His fate.* Crucifixion was their calculated way to kill the Jesus movement. They didn't simply want Jesus killed; they wanted Him killed in the most horrific manner possible—to deter anyone from continuing to follow Him. They weren't simply killing a Man, they were killing a movement. And they knew crucifixion would do the job. But instead of killing the movement, the cross seemed to *unleash* it. Why? There's only one reasonable explanation: Jesus rose from the dead!

2. If Jesus *didn't* resurrect from the grave, why were the disciples suddenly willing to die for Him after His death?

While Jesus was *alive*, they struggled to keep their courage. For example, when Jesus was arrested, the disciples fled at the prospect of being hauled off and crucified with Him. But after He had been executed, they were suddenly filled with boldness and showed they were willing to die courageously for His name. What could explain such a dramatic turnaround? There's only one reasonable explanation for their courage: Jesus rose from the dead!

3. If Jesus *didn't* resurrect from the grave, why didn't the Jewish leaders launch a search for His corpse?

Jesus' disciples claimed that He resurrected from the grave, and the most reasonable thing for the Jews to do in response would have been to launch a diligent search for the dead body. Why didn't they?

To back up a bit, you may recall the Jewish leaders placed a guard at the tomb to make sure Jesus' body wouldn't be stolen by His disciples. They didn't want the disciples to steal the body in the middle of the night and then claim He had resurrected, so they carefully placed a capable band of sentries to watch the tomb. After Jesus resurrected, an angel came and rolled the stone away, terrifying the sentinels to death and revealing an empty tomb. To cover the whole thing up, the Jewish leaders concocted a story that Jesus' disciples stole the corpse in the middle of the night while the guards slept. The disciples insisted, however, that Jesus had risen from the dead, and they were convincing huge crowds of followers of the truth of their claims.

The Jewish leaders were dismayed at the sudden momentum of the Jesus movement after His death, and they desperately wanted to kill it. To bury it, all they had to do was simply *produce a corpse*. A corpse would have dispersed the movement into oblivion,

The written accusation said He was King of the Jews. They crucified Him for the same reason the Father resurrected Him.

and the Jews knew it. They wanted Jesus' corpse so badly they could taste it. And here's the telling part: They didn't even *try* to find it. Had they believed their own story, they would have dispatched search parties until they found the body (it's not that easy to hide a corpse). But they didn't even *try*. Nor did the disciples try to hide one. There's only one reasonable explanation for all this: The Jewish leaders knew, deep down, that there was no corpse to be found. Jesus had risen from the dead!

In summary, Christ's resurrection is the only rational explanation for:

- The eruption of the Jesus movement after His death.
- The boldness of the disciples after His death.
- The fact that nobody was either hiding or searching for Jesus' corpse.

Christ arose!

After the Holy Spirit fell on the disciples, they preached the resurrection with chutzpah. When your leader dies but then resurrects back to life, it puts a certain grit in your spirit.

Resurrection Is Personal

Christ's crucifixion was exceedingly public—everybody saw it. But His resurrection was exceedingly private—nobody saw it. We might have expected the resurrection to happen with fireworks, pizzazz, and flare, but it was quite the opposite. Not a single person witnessed the moment when Jesus rose from the dead. Why not? Because the resurrection was a private affair between only three Persons—Father, Son, and Holy Spirit. They alone attended the event. It was too personal for the Father to share that moment with anyone else. "This one, Son, is between You and Me."

The crucifixion was personal to Jesus, the resurrection was personal to the Father. Let me explain.

Jesus took His crucifixion very personally. He cried, "My God, My God, why have You forsaken *ME*?" He considered the cross something the Father was doing to Him personally. When You have nails in Your hands and feet, You take it personally.

The same is true for you. When you're crucified with Christ, you look at God and say things like, "You've taken me down. You've caused me to eat dust. You removed me from my office. You've caused men to ride over me. You've separated me from my friends. You've confined and hemmed me in. You didn't hide deep darkness from my face. You've changed my times and seasons. I have unceasing sorrow. You've shut me up so that I cannot get out. Yes, I'm taking this personally."

And He means for you to take it personally. The cross knocks the business out of you and makes the whole thing personal.[1]

Then, when the Father resurrected Jesus, He was showing that the whole thing was personal for Him, too. He could have resurrected Jesus in a dramatic and public way that would have struck terror in the hearts of all His enemies, but instead He went private with it. The resurrection was too personal and intimate to be shared with anyone else. The Father was saying to His Son, "I'm Yours, and You're Mine" (see Acts 13:33). It was quite the exclusive affair.

God crucifies you to make it personal for you; then He resurrects you to show that the whole thing was personal for Him, too.

For more on the resurrection, come to the next chapter.

> When Christ arose as the *firstfruits* (1 Cor 15:20), He rose as the first of many. We now resurrect through the pathway He opened.

For Group Study and Discussion

1. Why was the resurrection essential to the cross story? What has the Lord taught you about this? Talk again about the statement, *The cross is never meant to be the last chapter of your story.*

2. *The agonizing part of the story is the most compelling chapter in the story.* Can you tell the story of someone alive today whose life illustrates that truth?

3. What do you consider to be one of the most compelling reasons to believe that Jesus rose from the dead?

4. Why do you think the resurrection was so quiet, so low-key, so non-dramatic? (in the sense that nobody saw it)

5. Has God ever done anything in your life that made your walk with Him intensely *personal*? Would you want to tell us about it?

6. As you close, pray in faith from Romans 6:5.

CHAPTER TWENTY-TWO

God Prefers Resurrection

Paul wrote that, at the resurrection, Jesus was "declared to be the Son of God with power according to the Spirit of holiness, by the resurrection from the dead" (Rom 1:4). Notice that Jesus was resurrected "with power according to the Spirit of holiness." In other words, He rose from hell because of holiness. David agreed, saying that God would not allow His *Holy One* to see corruption (Ps 16:10). Holiness got Him crucified, and then holiness got Him resurrected. In other words, the thing that got Him in got Him out.

That reminds me of Joseph. His holiness got him into prison and also got him out. Applied to your life, if obedience got you crucified, it'll also get you resurrected.

Identity

In Romans 1:4, Paul said the resurrection was a statement by the Father. We see this in his usage of the word, *declared*. The Greek word for *declared* means *to mark out*. At the resurrection, it's as though God took a heavenly highlighter, drew heavy circles around Jesus, and declared to all creation, "This one. This one is My Son."

The word *declared* indicates that the Father actually spoke something over Jesus when He raised Him from the dead. What did He say? Acts 13:33 tells us: "You are My Son." Resurrection was a statement. God was using a megaphone to announce to the universe the Person He was most loyal to. He even threw in an earthquake to underscore the message (Matt 27:51).

Resurrection must have infused Jesus with a rush of identity. *You're My Son.* Crucifixion was a crushing of identity, and resurrection was an infusion of

Anyone who can raise Himself from the dead can raise me up, too!

identity. Paul was helping us see, in Romans 1:4, that resurrection is all about *identity*.

Jesus never found His identity in the cross. He never said, "I am the crucifixion and the death," but rather, "I am the resurrection and the life" (John 11:25). He found His identity in resurrection—it's who He is. Resurrection isn't an event, as though it's something that happens to you; resurrection is a Person. When you're resurrected from your pit, you're having an encounter with a Person—because resurrection is who He is.

Your fiery trial will likely include a crushing of identity, because God is using your trial to shake everything in your life that can be shaken, identity included. He'll show you how you've found your identity in things that can be taken from you. This will help you anchor your identity in things that can't be shaken.

During the crucifixion, the Jews reviled Jesus by attacking His identity. They said, "If You are the Son of God, come down from the cross" (Matt 27:40). The same thing will probably happen to you, too. When you're being crushed, demonic voices will question who you are in Christ. "You say you're His beloved, but it's time to get in reality. Look—He's forsaken you. How can you call yourself His favorite when He's paying no attention to your voice?"

If you feel like you're going through hell, well, hell is the ultimate crushing of identity. Even Satan's identity will be crushed in the lake of fire (Isa 14:16). When Jesus descended to hell and preached to the souls in prison, the big question concerned His identity. "Who is this Preacher? Is He who He claims to be? Is it believable to suppose that He can save us?"

At the resurrection, the Father got out His highlighter, drew arrows around Jesus, and declared, "This is the one. This is My Son. This one is My favorite." When the Father declared His name, raised Him up, and gave Him all authority in heaven and earth, confidence must have coursed through His entire being. One of the things that's striking about Jesus, in the book of Revelation, is how confident He is in His identity. Little wonder—after the way the Father raised Him up!

Your journey to an anchored identity may be similar. Your trial may gut your sense of identity, but your resurrection will restore, confirm, and seal it. Resurrection comes with a rush of God-infused identity. Because you shared in His death, now you'll share in His resurrection from the dead.

You shall rise again!

God Prefers Resurrection

As we continue to explore the symbiotic relationship between crucifixion and resurrection, I want to state very clearly: *God values crucifixion, but He prefers resurrection.*

This principle is found in Romans 8:34, "It is Christ who died, and furthermore is also risen." The Greek word for *furthermore* means, *even better than that, to be desired even more than that.* The verse is saying this: "Christ died, but even better than that, He is also risen." His crucifixion was important and valuable, but His resurrection was even *better.*

The first part of our statement was, *God values crucifixion.* But why? Because He knows all the good things that can come from the crushing. For example, when we're in an excruciating trial, He's maturing us, perfecting us in holiness, refining our character, deepening our intimacy with Him, strengthening our faith, broadening our understanding in His word, and preparing us for more effective service.

But as much as He values all the good things being developed in us in our crucifixion, He prefers our resurrection.

Therefore, you need not wonder, "God, are You wanting to raise me up? Do You intend to lift me from this pit?" He's given us His answer in Romans 8:34. He desires your resurrection even more than your crushing.

Let the assurance of Romans 8:34 fill you with this confidence: God really *wants* to raise you up!

> The cross is the template for your journey in God.

Did Jesus Suffer in Hell?

Scripture doesn't tell us specifically whether Jesus suffered in hell, so my answer falls into the realm of conjecture. With that qualifier, I want to offer four reasons why I believe Jesus *didn't* suffer in hell.

1. On the cross, He said, "It is finished!" (John 19:30).

Jesus said this as He was dying. Those words indicated the fight was over and the price paid in full. If He needed to suffer even further in hell in order to procure our salvation, He might have said something like, "Almost finished!" But His statement rang with finality, "It is finished!" The suffering was over.

2. Death was His low point.

In his famous *kenosis*[1] passage, Paul described the emptying and humiliation of Christ in this manner:

> Who, being in the form of God, did not consider it robbery to be equal with God, but made Himself of no reputation, taking the form of a bondservant, and coming in the likeness of men. And being found in appearance as a man, He humbled Himself and became obedient to the point of death, even the death of the cross. Therefore God also has highly exalted Him and given Him the name which is above every name (Phil 2:6-9).

This passage describes a progressive humbling. "Equal with God...no reputation...a bondservant...obedient to death...the cross." With each phrase, Paul showed how Jesus humbled Himself lower, lower, lower. The lowest point in His self-emptying was "the death of the cross." Even though He descended from the cross to hell, the lowest point mentioned by Paul was not hell but His death. From the moment He

---

1   In Philippians 2:7, Paul used the Greek word *kenosis* which means *emptying*. The NAS rendering is more accurate: "but emptied Himself, taking the form of a bond-servant."

expired, He began His stride forward toward resurrection. Since death was His low point, it seems His suffering ended at His expiration on the cross.

3. David said Jesus was glad in Sheol. (Sheol is the Hebrew equivalent of hell.)

David wrote prophetically of Christ's descent to Sheol with these words: "Therefore my heart is glad, and my glory rejoices; my flesh also will rest in hope. For You will not leave my soul in Sheol, nor will You allow Your Holy One to see corruption" (Ps 16:9-10). When Jesus descended to hell, His body rested "in hope" in the grave over the course of the Sabbath (the day of rest). While His soul was in hell, David described Him as saying, "My heart is glad." Why was He glad? Because He knew the Father was going to resurrect Him before corruption (decay) would begin to decompose His entombed corpse. (Corpses typically start to decay after three days.)

Jesus had a glad heart in hell. Never before had hell hosted a happy heart. Sheol had no idea what to do with Gladheart.

Since Jesus was glad in hell, I take that to mean He was not submerged by its sorrows and torments, but had completed His sufferings on the cross. Although in hell, He was victor over its hopeless torments.

4. He preached in hell.

Speaking of Christ's descension to hell, Peter said He "went and preached to the spirits in prison" (1 Pet 3:19). He preached the gospel to imprisoned spirits held by the power of Death and Hades.

I can't imagine Jesus being able to preach effectively and persuasively to hell's prisoners if He Himself were also subject to its torments. How could spirits in prison believe His message if He were

At the tomb, the guards were scared to death by the life they encountered—because you just don't expect to see eternal life in a cemetery.

as powerless in Hades as they?

Furthermore, I don't think hell gives out preaching permits. Satan didn't want Jesus preaching down there, and would have stopped Him if he could. The fact that Jesus was preaching unhindered demonstrated He had authority in hell over Satan and his demons. When in Hades, Jesus wasn't under its power but Lord over it.

Did Jesus suffer in hell? I'm voting no.

Someone might think an exploration of this question is meaningless and speculative, but I find it highly significant. During the approximate thirty-six hours (give or take) that Jesus was in Hades, my soul envisions a brewing storm. All of hell's demons were frantic because they had no control over Holy Gladheart. Nothing was going according to their plan.

During His time in Hades, Jesus walked about freely as a victorious Champion who triggered a rumble everywhere He strode. As He made preparations for the greatest jail break of cosmic history, hell's powers were in convulsions.

When Christ began to rise from the dead, it triggered shock waves that reached the deepest recesses of hell's corridors. The *hellquake* reached all the way to the surface and triggered an *earthquake* (Matt 27:51). The ascent from hell was drama on steroids, and one day I look forward to watching that episode in heaven's virtual library.

All this leads to my next question.

When Did Jesus Bruise Satan's Head?

Let me explain the context to that question.

In the garden of Eden, the Father spoke to Satan about the cross and said, "He shall bruise your head, and you shall bruise His heel" (Gen 3:15). He told Satan that Jesus would bruise his head, and that he would bruise Jesus' heel. Satan bruised Jesus' heel on the cross in a *literal* way when His feet were nailed to the wood. Additionally, Satan bruised Jesus' heel in a *figurative* sense, meaning that Satan hurt Him in only a secondary or minor way. (An injury to the heel is not fatal.) Jesus' wounds on the cross were real and strong, but in the grand scheme of things they were as insignificant as the bruising of a heel.

In contrast, the Father told Satan that Jesus would bruise his head. A blow to the head is much more devastating than a blow to the heel. Jesus suffered a blow that left a permanent scar, but Satan suffered a blow that left him permanently disabled.

Our question is, *when* did Jesus lay that blow to Satan's head? The standard answer is, *On the cross*, but then nobody can identify precisely how Jesus struck Satan on the cross. Personally, I don't think it happened on the cross. I have a different answer to submit for your consideration. I think Satan sustained the blow at the resurrection. Let me explain.

We said previously that Satan killed Jesus on the cross in the gamble that Death would be stronger than He had anticipated, and would be able to imprison Him forever. When Gladheart descended to hell in holiness and demonstrated authority over its torments, Satan was frantic. Jesus was demonstrating a power over Death he hadn't anticipated.

Satan knew that if Jesus should resurrect from the dead, his defeat would be final and comprehensive. When Jesus began to ascend from hell, therefore, Satan was desperate to stop Him. His eternal fate was at stake! Death wasn't stopping Him, and the gates of hell weren't containing Him. *Yikes!* Something had to be done. This upward movement toward resurrection had to be stopped! With Hades and Death impotent to stop Christ's rise, it seems Satan's only option was to place himself between Jesus and hell's gates. I believe Satan *personally and physically* tried to stop Him from breaking out of hell.

When he attempted physical contact with Jesus, that's when the hit came. Jesus leveled a blow to the head of the adversary that left him bloodied and incapacitated.

There were two earthquakes because, at His death, the way into the Holiest was ripped open, and at His resurrection, the way out of Hades was ripped open.

Satan lay helplessly in a wounded heap while Jesus and His captives marched from hell and resurrected in Holy Spirit power.

At the cross, Satan confronted the Lamb; at the resurrection, he encountered the Lion.

Jesus bruised his head (Gen 3:15), divested him of his armor (Col 2:15), took the keys of Hades and Death (Rev 1:18), plundered hell, and rose on the third day. Then He divided the spoils in fulfillment of Ephesians 4:8, "When He ascended on high, He led captivity captive, and gave gifts to men."

The plan was not to invade hell from the outside, but to defeat it from the inside.[2]

You don't need a key to get into Hades, but you do need one to get out. His resurrection proved He has the keys.

Resurrection is the high water mark, in all Scripture, of God's power released on earth. When extolling the greatness of God's power, Paul didn't point to the creation of the universe, but to the resurrection of Christ:

> And what is the exceeding greatness of His power toward us who believe, according to the working of His mighty power which He worked in Christ when He raised Him from the dead and seated Him at His right hand in the heavenly places, far above all principality and power and might and dominion, and every name that is named, not only in this age but also in that which is to come (Eph 1:19-21).

Today I praise the mighty power of God! We still don't know how strong He is. All we know is, He's stronger than Death and hell. Our Champion, the Son of David, bested the Goliaths of the underworld: Death, Hades, and Satan. Praise His name!

Therefore, it matters not how deep your pit may be. Set your hope on Christ, for He has the keys to *your* resurrection, too.

---

2   Go deeper on this idea in my book, *Opened From the Inside.*

For Group Study and Discussion

1. The resurrection was the Father identifying His Son. Has God ever raised you up in a way that infused you with identity? Tell us about it. Ch. 23

2. *God values crucifixion, but He prefers resurrection.* How does that statement encourage you in your journey?

3. Did Jesus suffer in hell? Study that question this week, and bring your insights and Scriptures to the group discussion.

4. Talk about the author's theory that Jesus bruised Satan's head as He was resurrecting from Hades. Do you agree or disagree? Can we also expect to bloody the head of our adversary?

5. As you close, center your prayers and praise around Ephesians 1:19-21.

CHAPTER TWENTY-THREE
Resurrection Completed the Connection

I've been working this entire book to make my way toward this final point: Resurrection made available to us everything Christ labored to purchase on the cross. Here's our verse for this:

> And if Christ is not risen, your faith is futile; you are still in your sins! (1 Cor 15:17).

This verse says that, if Christ had died on the cross and descended to hell but not risen again, our faith in the cross would be futile, and we would still be in our sins. The implications of this statement are *huge*.

Jesus labored mightily on the cross to pay the price for the forgiveness of our sins, for the healing of our bodies, for health in our souls, and for our eternal companionship. When He cried, "It is finished," He meant that the price was paid in full. Calvary's work was complete, and Jesus descended to hell in holiness.

However, if death had been strong enough to hold Him and Jesus had not risen from the dead, nothing purchased on the cross would be ours. Although paid for, all those benefits would have been lost.

Like a Closed Circuit

For an illustration of this, imagine that you ordered and paid for a truckload of product from a manufacturer. But during the trip, the truck got run off the road and never got to its destination. All the product in the truck belonged to you because you paid for it, but none of it actually arrived to your place. That scenario illustrates, in a weak way, what would have happened if Christ had died but not resurrected.

The product (our salvation) would have been paid for, but it would have never arrived to make a difference in our lives.

Or consider the example of an electric switch. A switch in an electrical circuit serves to connect the power of the utility company to your appliances or lights. According to this illustration, the cross provided the electrical power we needed for all our lights to come on, and the resurrection was the switch. Just as the flipping of a switch closes an electrical circuit and sends the power to our lights, resurrection lit up our lives with all of the cross's power. If Jesus had died but not resurrected, we would be unable to access the power of the cross but would still be lost in our sins.

In other words, the cross by itself wasn't enough to save us. We needed both cross and resurrection.

Think about the ramifications of this verse—they're stunning. If Christ had borne the stripes on His back for our healing; if He wore the crown of thorns and became a curse to liberate us from the curse of the law; if he had taken the nails in His hands and feet and shed His blood for the forgiveness of our sins; if He had absorbed the chastisement for our griefs and sorrows so we could enjoy His peace; if He had cried, "It is finished," because the price was paid in full; if the Father had seen the labor of His soul and been satisfied; if He had expired, been buried, descended to hell, and preached in hell to the souls in prison—but then *not risen*—everything accomplished in the cross would have been in vain. We would still be in our sins.

Christ's resurrection was *essential*. Without it, we would experience no healing, no salvation, and no eternal life. Crucifixion had to be crowned and consummated by resurrection.

Resurrection was like a cosmic circuit breaker. When Jesus rose from the dead, all the lights came on. All the power of the gospel suddenly connected to our planet,

> The angel rolled back the tombstone not to let Jesus out but to let us in.

and our destinies were forever changed. The cross purchased it, and the resurrection delivered it.

Without resurrection, the cross would have been like a dud bomb that never detonated. Together with resurrection, the cross became a nuclear explosion that split eternity.

Resurrection has cosmic implications for our entire globe, but it also carries great meaning for your personal journey in God. Let me show you what I mean.

Your Resurrection Releases the Power of Your Story

When you're in a fiery trial, you're fighting and laboring for many things—just like Jesus did on the cross. Here are some of the things you're laboring to attain through your fiery trial:

- You want to buy the gold of Christlikeness in the fire so that you become more like Him.
- You're pressing into a deeper understanding of His ways and purposes in the trials of life.
- You're chasing after mountain-moving faith.
- You want intimacy with Jesus that's real and fruitful.
- You desire to be so full of the Holy Spirit that He can manifest Himself freely through your life.
- You're devouring the word for greater understanding so that you can become an overcomer and a messenger to your generation.
- You're qualifying for a higher rank in the kingdom so you can expend yourself even more extravagantly in servanthood.
- You're fighting for a testimony so that your story will witness to all generations of God's faithfulness and goodness.

All this, and more! These are some of the things you're

laboring for in your crucifixion.

But if you labor for all these great attainments and then are not raised up, all that you've labored to attain will be comparatively ineffectual—that is, it will not be made available to the body of Christ in a lifegiving way.

Just as Christ's resurrection was essential to His labors, so is yours. In your trial, you've been laboring and gathering, and God's been doing wonderful things in your heart and life. But one thing is still lacking: your resurrection. For the story to be complete, you must be resurrected from your pit.

Resurrection Is Essential!

Paul used the word *futile* in 1 Corinthians 15:17. He said that without resurrection the cross would have been *futile*. In the same sense, everything you've attained in your trial will be *futile* unless you're raised up from it. To say it another way, if you're not raised up, the body of Christ will dismiss and forget your story. What God wanted to birth will be like a stillborn child, and His intended end will not be realized (Isa 26:18). Your testimony will be silenced.

Again, here's the point: *Your resurrection is essential!* When God raises you up, everything you've labored and fought for in the duress of your adversity will become available to the body of Christ. Suddenly, like the throwing of a switch, your story will light up a generation.

It bears repeating: The cross is never meant to be your last chapter. The story in God's heart is never complete until you've been raised up in victory over your trial. Let the faith of God fill your heart right now because God wants to raise you up. He prefers your resurrection!

Paul gave us a principle in this same chapter about Christ's example that's valuable to understand:

When God resurrects the One you've crucified, wisdom would suggest you do a little inventory.

> For if the dead do not rise, then Christ is not risen....But now
> Christ is risen from the dead, and has become the firstfruits of
> those who have fallen asleep (1 Cor 15:16, 20).

The idea of *firstfruits* is that He was the first of many to resurrect. Here's the principle: *As the first of many, every attainment of Christ is now also available to you. If He did it, so can you.* In other words, the death and resurrection of Christ was not a unique, one-off, one-of-a-kind event that was never to be repeated; rather, it was a template for your journey. He did the cross to show you how to do your cross, and He resurrected so that you can, too. As the firstfruits, Jesus' example prophesies resurrection over your future. Get ready for resurrection!

Resurrection Takes the Story Viral

God wants to raise you up from your pit of adversity. The stakes are so huge that hell will do everything in its power to fight your resurrection. Hell helps your crucifixion along (just as it helped Christ's to happen), but it will do its utmost to resist your resurrection. Just as Satan personally resisted Christ's resurrection (and took a deadly blow to the head as a consequence), he will also resist yours. The war is over your *resurrection.*

Why? Because resurrection will take the story viral. If you're raised up, an entire generation will be shaped, empowered, strengthened, enabled, and instructed. Through your endurance, they'll gain courage to endure in their own God-story. Everything hinges on resurrection.

Do you realize why you're in your current trial? God chose you because He saw the makings of a great story. You've got the angels and all of heaven cheering you on and rooting for your resurrection.

Fight! Finish your course! Lay hold of resurrection power.

When a saint gets buried in a prison, the warfare around

that saint goes stratospheric. If they die in that prison, the story is muted and disappears. But if they rise from that prison, the story becomes an explosive witness that shifts things in the Spirit for many others. Again, the stakes around resurrection are enormous.

The cross and resurrection of Christ are the first and great example of this principle. But the Bible is chock full of other examples that illustrate the same truth. Let me mention just a few.

Consider Sarah, Hannah, and Elizabeth, who share some common elements in their stories: All three were unable to bear children, they were greatly distressed by their barrenness, they cried to God for a son, He heard their cry, healed them, and gave them each a miracle baby boy. Their barrenness was akin to their crucifixion; birthing a baby boy was akin to their resurrection. Had they never received a miracle baby, we would have never known of their existence. But because they were raised up by God into motherhood, their testimony has strengthened the faith of many generations. Their resurrection took the story viral.

Consider Joseph. What if Joseph had died in prison? Someone might have tried to comfort him by telling him that he could still enjoy God's presence in his prison, and he could have a powerful ministry of serving the other inmates and interpreting their dreams. But that would pale in contrast to what God intended to do though Joseph's life. God wanted to redeem Joseph's prison and change the destiny of nations. The truth is, if Joseph had died in prison, we wouldn't have even heard the story. None of his suffering would have had relevance to us. But because he rose from the prison to the palace, his life speaks volumes to prisoners *everywhere*. Now, saints of all ages have gained courage and faith from the example of Joseph's prison.

Consider David. What if David had stayed in Ziklag and never been raised to

> The cross displayed Christ's humanity and the resurrection His divinity.

the throne of Israel? We would have never heard of him. He labored for years as an outcast to attain some profound things in the Spirit, but the only reason we benefit from those things today is because he was raised to the throne. Resurrection took his story viral.

Consider Job. What if he had not been healed and raised up by God? We would have no book by his name, and we would have never heard of the man. But his resurrection took his story viral, and now every generation receives comfort from the legacy of his fatherhood.

Consider Moses. The only reason we know his story is because God raised him up from a wilderness of obscurity and made him the primary leader of the nation of Israel. Resurrection took his story viral.

Consider Abraham. If he had never received his miracle baby, Isaac, we would have never heard of him. But because God raised him up into fatherhood, his witness has rocked human history.

Now it's *your* turn. Do you feel buried in a prison, or do you feel like your life is being poured out like water? Take hold of the resurrected Savior's hand. He who was raised up by God also wants to carry you, strengthen you, and raise you up as well. Your resurrection will take *your* story viral.

Resurrection Is in Your DNA

Believe in His resurrection power! This is what the cross of Christ thunders to us today. Jesus isn't trying to help you cope with your cross so you can expire with a good attitude; He's empowering you to endure in faith so you can lay hold of resurrection.

Jesus called us *sons of the resurrection* (Luke 20:36). That means you have resurrection in your DNA. It's imprinted into the binary code of your hard drive. You can't get away from it—resurrection throbs in your soul. You carry an unwavering assurance that God fulfills all His promises. For you, resurrection is inexorable, inevitable, and unstoppable. Sons of the resurrection inevitably inherit resurrection. They refuse to be denied.

Therefore, embrace God's promises and hold out for resurrection! Christ's resurrection announces, *There's more where that came from.* His resurrection was not the great finale, but rather the great inception—the first of many. Resurrection is the inheritance of all God's children, so go after it. Pursue "any means," therefore, to "attain to the resurrection from the dead" (Phil 3:11).

> Resurrection isn't an event but a Person.

For Group Study and Discussion

1. Take time this week to study 1 Corinthians 15:17. Bring your insights and supporting Scriptures to the discussion. What does this verse mean to you?

2. How did the illustration of an electric switch help you understand the power of the resurrection better?

3. Did this chapter strengthen your faith to believe God for your own resurrection? Tell us what you're believing God for.

4. As our firstfruits, Jesus did it first so we could experience the same thing. What are some things Jesus experienced that you're expecting to also experience?

5. *The war is over your resurrection.* In what way have you experienced hell resisting your resurrection?

6. This chapter mentioned the stories of several heroes: Sarah, Hannah, Elizabeth, Joseph, David, Job, Moses, and Abraham. Which of these stories might be a favorite of yours, and why?

7. As you close, let Philippians 3:8-11 guide and ignite your prayers.

CHAPTER TWENTY-FOUR

Courage

I've endeavored throughout this book to reveal the cross of Christ. Have you seen it? If so, it will fill you with holy courage to follow the crucified Savior.

The cross gives courage.

Peter Eventually Found His Courage

Before His arrest, Jesus predicted that Peter would deny Him three times, but Peter vehemently insisted, "Even if I have to die with You, I will not deny You!" (Matt 26:35). He was persuaded he had the courage to die with Jesus, but when Jesus was arrested and put on trial, his valor vaporized, and he denied his association with Jesus.

After Peter denied for the third time that he knew Jesus, a rooster crowed, and Jesus looked at him. Realizing he had just fulfilled Jesus' prediction, he went out and wept bitterly (Luke 22:62).

Peter wept for two reasons. First, he wept because he had failed Jesus by denying Him three times. But more than that, he wept because he realized he didn't have the courage to go back in there, man up, and confess that Jesus was his Master. Had he possessed the mettle, he could have gathered himself, stood up and said, "Guys, I wasn't honest. The truth is, I'm one of His disciples. I've got to own up to it. I'm with Him." But he couldn't do it. He simply didn't have the reserves in his soul to reverse things and make it right. When the heat was on, his courage collapsed.

As with Peter, the cross will test *our* courage.

Mind you, Peter's story has a happy ending. When the Holy Spirit was poured out at Pentecost, the Spirit infused him with holy boldness and instantly turned him into a man of uncommon courage (Acts 2). The Spirit made him so fearless that he uttered one of the most courageous, politically-incorrect, intentionally-inflammatory statements in all Scripture. Take time for the whole story:

> Now as they spoke to the people, the priests, the captain of the temple, and the Sadducees came upon them, being greatly disturbed that they taught the people and preached in Jesus the resurrection from the dead. And they laid hands on them, and put them in custody until the next day, for it was already evening. However, many of those who heard the word believed; and the number of the men came to be about five thousand. And it came to pass, on the next day, that their rulers, elders, and scribes, as well as Annas the high priest, Caiaphas, John, and Alexander, and as many as were of the family of the high priest, were gathered together at Jerusalem. And when they had set them in the midst, they asked, "By what power or by what name have you done this?" Then Peter, filled with the Holy Spirit, said to them, "Rulers of the people and elders of Israel: If we this day are judged for a good deed done to a helpless man, by what means he has been made well, let it be known to you all, and to all the people of Israel, that by the name of Jesus Christ of Nazareth, whom you crucified, whom God raised from the dead, by Him this man stands here before you whole. This is the 'stone which was rejected by you builders, which has become the chief cornerstone.' Nor is there salvation in any other, for there is no other name under heaven given among men by which we must be saved." Now when they saw the boldness of Peter and John, and perceived that they were uneducated and untrained men, they marveled. And they realized that they had been with Jesus (Acts 4:1-13).

I say that Peter's statement here is exceedingly inflammatory because:

- He meant for his statement to be made known not only to the leaders who were present, but also to the entire nation of Israel—at a time when the leaders were doing everything in their

> Bow now before the Lamb so you can stand later before the Lion.

power to quell the spread of the resurrection message.

- The leaders who were present were the same ones who had presided at Jesus' trial just a few days earlier (Matt 26:57). By assembling the same court, the implicit message was, *We're the guys who had enough clout to get Jesus crucified, and we'll use it again if we have to.* Peter read the threat implicitly and yet didn't cower in the least.
- He accused them to their face of crucifying the Man whom God raised from the dead. (When God raises the Man you've just crucified, it should give you some pause.)
- He testified that salvation is to be found in no one else except Jesus of Nazareth, "for there is no other name under heaven given among men by which we must be saved." It was impossible to be more politically incorrect in that moment.

The risen Christ had given him courage.
Now let's look at a second example of courage.

Joseph of Arimathea Found Courage

The cross put courage in the soul of Joseph of Arimathea. Here's the verse for it:

> Joseph of Arimathea, a prominent council member, who was himself waiting for the kingdom of God, coming and taking courage, went in to Pilate and asked for the body of Jesus (Mark 15:43).

Joseph was from the town of Arimathea, and he was "a prominent council member" which means he was a member of the *Sanhedrin*. The Sanhedrin was the seventy-member supreme court of Jewish politics and religion. It sat at the top rung of the ladder of Jewish society. In other words, Joseph had climbed his way to the apex of his career. Furthermore, being *prominent* among the seventy members, he was a leader of leaders. His role in the Sanhedrin gave him prestige, reputation, influence, power, and honor, and last but not least, money.

The Sanhedrin was vehemently opposed to Jesus, and they played a primary role in securing His crucifixion. During Jesus' earthly ministry, the Sanhedrin had made it very clear that anyone in their ranks who became a believer in Jesus as their Messiah would be expelled from the court and shunned.

Joseph had listened to Jesus carefully, watched His ministry, and had come to believe in Him. However, he remained silent about his faith because he knew that, if he went public with it, he would lose *everything*—including favor, position, income, and career. So he remained quiet and kept his thoughts to himself.

The cross changed all that. When Joseph saw the extravagance of Jesus' self-sacrifice on the cross, he decided to go all in. Going to Pilate, he asked permission to bury the body. By burying Jesus, he was making a public statement: *I'm with Jesus of Nazareth.* With that act, he was probably forfeiting his career, income, popularity, and influence. What made him willing to hazard all of that? The cross. Seeing it gave him the courage he needed to go public with his faith.

When you truly see the cross, it gives you courage—courage to take a public stand for Christ.

As you've read this book, have you seen the cross? Has His courage inspired yours? He who had the courage to die for you will also give you the courage to die for Him. But losing your life you'll find it.

When you go public with your faith, Jesus Himself owns you and says, "Whoever confesses Me before men, him I will also confess before My Father who is in heaven" (Matt 10:32). And He adds, "I will raise him up at the last day" (John 6:40).

Your biggest decision in life will be how to respond to the crucifixion of Jesus Christ.

Jesus demonstrated His loyalty to the Father by going to the cross, and now He invites you to demonstrate your loyalty to His cross. When you go public with your faith in the midst of an unbelieving world, He says to you, "I will never forget this, but I will raise you up at the last day."

Today I invite you to swear your head to the cross of Jesus Christ and tell the world about it. He'll never forget.

A Prayer

Jesus, I believe in Your cross. I believe that You suffered, died, were buried, descended to hell, resurrected, and ascended to heaven. I'm standing up to declare my faith before everyone I know. I'm going to talk about Your cross all the time. Fill me with Your Holy Spirit and give me the power to stand courageously in my generation. May I be conformed to Your death so that I may attain to the resurrection from the dead. Amen.

Date:

Your Signature:

Books by Bob Sorge

Secrets of the Secret Place Curriculum
- *Secrets of the Secret Place* (paperback & hardcover)
- *Secrets of the Secret Place: Companion Study Guide*
- Secrets 12-part Video Series
- Leaders Manual

Prayer
Reset: 20 Ways to a Consistent Prayer Life
Unrelenting Prayer
Illegal Prayers
Power of the Blood
Minute Meditations

Worship
Exploring Worship: A Practical Guide to Praise and Worship
Glory: When Heaven Invades Earth
Following The River: A Vision For Corporate Worship
Next Wave: Worship in a New Era

Enduring Faith
In His Face
The Fire Of Delayed Answers
The Fire Of God's Love
Pain, Perplexity, & Promotion: A Prophetic Interpretation of the Book of Job
Opened From the Inside: Taking the Stronghold of Zion
God's Still Writing Your Story
The Chastening of the Lord: The Forgotten Doctrine
The Cross: Never Too Dead for Resurrection

Leadership
Dealing With the Rejection and Praise of Man
Envy: The Enemy Within
Loyalty: The Reach Of The Noble Heart
It's Not Business It's Personal
A Covenant With My Eyes
Stuck: Help for the Troubled Home

For info on each title, go to oasishouse.com.

Bob's books are available at:
- Oasis House, 816-767-8880
- oasishouse.com
- christianbook.com
- amazon.com
- Kindle, iBooks, Nook, Google Play
- Audible

To stay connected:
YouTube/bobsorge
Instagram: bob.sorge
Blog: bobsorge.com
twitter.com/BOBSORGE
Facebook.com/BobSorgeMinistry